STOP
think
GO, DO

SH—For Louise and Nick
MI—For Nicky, Zoe, and Ivo

First published in the United States of America in 2012 by
Rockport Publishers, a member of
Quayside Publishing Group
100 Cummings Center
Suite 406-L
Beverly, Massachusetts 01915-6101
Telephone: (978) 282-9590
Fax: (978) 283-2742
www.rockpub.com
www.rockpaperink.com

10 9 8 7 6 5 4 3 2

ISBN: 978-1-59253-766-2

Digital edition published in 2012
eISBN: 978-1-61058-389-3

Library of Congress Cataloging-in-Publication Data is available.

Design: Landers Miller Design
Cover Design: Landers Miller Design

Printed in China

STOP
think
GO, DO

HOW TYPOGRAPHY & GRAPHIC DESIGN
INFLUENCE BEHAVIOR

STEVEN HELLER & MIRKO ILIĆ

Rockport Publishers
100 Cummings Center, Suite 406L
Beverly, MA 01915

rockpub.com • rockpaperink.com

CONTENTS

1

INFORM

Graphic design focuses
our eyes and mind
on what is already
instinctively hardwired.

2

ADVOCATE

The language of advocacy
has a common goal: alter
behavior and act upon
instincts, whatever the
outcome may be.

3

PLAY

Play adds dimension
to design, enabling the
viewer to have more
active participation in it.

4

CAUTION

Cautionary messages
force the receiver to
go somewhere or do
something to avoid
dangerous consequences.

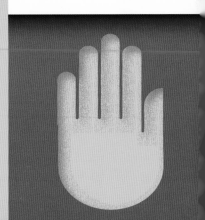

STOP GO READ THIS →

HERE'S A FACT OF LIFE: YOU ARE CONSTANTLY BEING TOLD WHAT TO DO.

Don't deny it! (See?!) At all times, somewhere, someone is sending you overt and covert messages, often through media designed to control your behavior (and now there's more media than ever). In the film version of George Orwell's *1984* (with Richard Burton in his last role), the ubiquitous "Big Brother is Watching You" poster makes clear that on- and off-screen, Big Brother *is* always present.

This infamous saying was not a benign greeting from a benevolent "brother," but an official command to *obey*—or face the consequences. It was like all those posters we saw in school, telling us to do this and not do that—even the ones about staying healthy were rendered in a threatening tone and ominous style. Of course, Orwell's novel was about a fictional totalitarian nation, Oceania, and a faux omniscient leader, but too many real governments—past and present—have Big Brothers, or shall we call them demagogues. This gives credence to the fact that we are routinely told when, where, and how to behave—for reasonable and irrational reasons. We accept these dicta virtually without question.

Now, read on! Or else!

Many of our daily commands are communicated in the forms of graphic, environmental, and product design. We are conditioned to respond to the controlling missives we receive, and not inconsequentially, by the illustrative and typographic appearance of those missives.

Take the everyday act of crossing the street: It is dictated by terse commands—*stop, go, cross, don't cross. Alt!* Whatever the language, the orders are always comprehensible in print. If not the specific words (*berhenti* means "stop" in Malaysia)—or the alphabet (Cyrillic or Chinese)—then the colors (e.g., red for stop, yellow for wait, green for go), symbols (e.g., outstretched hands for stop), and sign shapes are often unmistakable indicators. There is a wide range of *forbidden* (*verbotten*), *beware*, and scores of iterations of *never ever* or *never again* messages presented to us in picture and word—some of them are official, others are ad hoc—found everywhere.

Street signs are not the only graphic interventions that impact our behavioral consciousness and subconsciousness. Our lives are filled with typographic and pictorial decrees and warnings designed to either regiment, protect, or otherwise condition the everyday. So common (even inconsequential) are some, we often take them for granted—and might even ignore them entirely (who knows what *post no bills* actually means, or *employees must wash hands* doesn't apply to me). Other times they are so jarring (like the unambiguous word *quarantine*) we cannot skirt the implication, even if we tried. Short and lengthily worded commands, proclamations, testimonies, and directions have been essential to our hardwired behavior since signs and symbols were first scratched onto the Lascaux caves. "Watch Out for Wooly Mammoths!"

Designing commands is not, however, the exclusive province of graphic designers. In fact, when words are used to influence behavior, the niceties of typographic design are often sacrificed for the brutish immediacy of pure, untutored expression. Of course, typography is essential in getting most messages across, and designers are responsible, at the very least, for designing the typefaces, if not also how they are used. It is unlikely that the word *stop* would be typeset in a curlicue script—it just doesn't have the authority—but anyone, designer or not, can select a slab serif or bold gothic face to make the word (or statement) "scream."

The term *scream* (or *screamer*) is, in fact, a jargonistic description referring to extra-large headlines usually on tabloid newspapers. It further refers to those words—and images—that demonstratively influence the receiver or audience. Designers are well equipped to make the right typographic decisions to achieve this primal scream. But nondesigners, and this includes graphic arts and non–graphic arts professionals, also possess a naive capacity to make fundamental selections that achieve their goal.

When design is operating best, the audience is less aware of the design tropes than how the design functions.

It is a fairly safe bet that if you want someone to take a message seriously, then you must (emphasis on *must*) draw the letters big and bold or select a typeface with those same characteristics. It doesn't take a master of fine arts to do it. But a master of letterforms will do it better than someone who is merely selecting random alphabets—or so we masters of letterforms want to believe. When manipulating (or influencing) behavior of any kind through print, on signs, or on LED screens, the words carry the "song," but type and image are the "melody." These design elements are hooks that make good lyrics into great music. This metaphor is apt, because what is music but a means of altering behavior and triggering emotion?

Design is symphonical, quietly melodical, romantically poetical, and let's not forget rousingly oratorical. Type and image, composition and arrangement, color and hue—choices that designers make all the time—can make a huge difference in how we receive the messages and, ultimately, take those persistent orders from others.

Admittedly, not all design is so demonstrative as to mandate behavioral submission or acquiescence. Decorative design is essentially more like wallpaper than a wall poster. Most book typography is meant to facilitate unhampered reading—it's not giving orders. Design is ostensibly a framing mechanism. In modernist terms, it makes order out of chaos. When design is operating best, the audience is less aware of the design tropes than how the design functions. And although we are obviously conscious of the look of things, the meaning of things is ultimately more important (well, most of the time).

The book you are about to consume (and *enjoy!*) is concerned with that aspect of graphic design that subsumes the look to the message, although look is of great importance regarding how the message is telegraphed and received. The genesis for this book derives from three different well-known design artifacts. Each, in its own way, demands attention and commands behavior:

1. The stop sign, discussed earlier, is the quintessential "attention grabber"; only the word *Achtung!* has equal force to make us "stop, look, and listen."
2. "Keep Calm and Carry On," the 1939 poster produced by the British Ministry of Information, initially intended to strengthen morale in the event of a wartime disaster. The designer is unknown and the poster was never really used. But it was resurrected recently and reproduced with a curiously calming effect.
3. "I Want You" is the 1917 James Montgomery Flagg poster showing Uncle Sam pointing his finger at potential recruits for World War I. The concept, based on other iterations in England, Germany, France, and Russia, effectively penetrated the collective psyche with graphic force.

Words and images fused together into a graphic artifact usually engender Pavlovian responses (show an ice-cold glass of beer under the word *BUD* and, if you like such libations, you will long for the taste). Each of the above examples forces us almost involuntarily to *think* and act—*stop* is a matter of safety; *keep calm* is a matter of sanity; and *I want you* is a matter of responsibility. We think and act according to our self-interest—and reflect after it is all over.

When Shepard Fairey created his now ubiquitous, generationally iconic *OBEY* brand, he was satirizing the power of design and advertising to demand obedience. Even the most liberal individual wants obedience from someone.

Of course, there is a range of critical responses to behavioral design. For this book the topics naturally organize into Inform, Advocate, Play, Caution, Entertain, Express, Educate, and Transform. You may (emphasis on *may*) ask, why these are the principles of this book. And we will tell you:

INFORM is, informatively, parallel to *educate* but not exactly the same. It involves tweaking the audience by bringing to light an issue, essence, or concern that requires contemplation.

....

ADVOCATE is, perhaps, the most common of all because designers are often called upon to create messages that rouse an audience to support and therefore engage in an issue or event.

....

PLAY is what every design does, whether knowingly or not. What is the moving around of word and image but a puzzle or game? This is the essence of the following sections; through play we learn, entertain, express, inform, and transform.

....

CAUTION is, doubtless, the most classic graphic design behavioral message genre. *Keep out, no trespassing, wrong way, beware of dog,* and other cautionary missives are designed to ensure health and well-being of one and all.

....

ENTERTAIN is, decidedly, the genre of behavioral design that everyone enjoys the most. No one is threatened by entertainment, which has various outcomes but one fundamental goal—to bring enjoyment.

....

EXPRESS is, curiously, the largest growth area, for more designers are using graphically designed words and slogans as a means of expressing personal beliefs, philosophies, and manifestoes with the goal of influencing others.

EDUCATE is, in fact, a combination of all the categories here, except specifically it is the rubric under which more detailed knowledge messages are shared.

....

TRANSFORM is an overlapping category whereby projects borne of play are transformations of what they originally appear to be. These pieces are sly and wicked, using visual puns and graphic manipulation to come in under the perception radar.

There are many shared traits between sections, but the constant throughout the work is playfulness—what Paul Rand called the "play-principle." When most effective, play entertains, but also implies the power and process of playing or experimenting with form and its impact on the audience.

Much of the design works or artifacts in this book are, more or less, driven by words. Although what we call behavioral or behavior-influencing design is not all words (sometimes pictures are indeed worth 1,000 or more words), the majority are not just word based but word and picture integrated. Some of the typography is simpler—more minimalist—than others that are elaborate—at times metaphorical. Images play a defining commanding role too, but only insofar as they are well integrated with the words and type.

Language is our foremost concern in this book. How the design language(s) formally and informally interact and intersect with a message in such a way that the audience's behavior is altered, the result being a passive or active response—but a behavioral response nonetheless.

Not all design tells you—or us—what to do or how to feel or when to think, but much design attempts to get under the skin and into the mind. This is a survey of some of the most effective of these over the past five years.

WE WANT YOU TO READ THIS BOOK! OH YES...NOW!

1

INSPIRE

UNDER STAND

ar•tic•u•late

INFORM

Graphic design focuses our eyes and mind on what is already instinctively hardwired.

"Knowledge is power," Sir Francis Bacon wrote in 1597. So, to inform an audience through designed messages is to impart knowledge, which enables self-condfidence and strength that leads to power. What better way to influence behavior than to inform. Right? Therefore, this book begins with a chapter devoted to designing frames for the presentation of valuable (and not so valuable) information. This is the broadest of the book's categories, since by definition the graphic designer's single most important job is to inform.

By processing information the receiver has the ability to stop, go, think, do—we hope.

Often, however, information is just so much noise, empty and unnecessary. Or it is propaganda, manipulated and untrue, but made to be important. Or it is a hawker's pitch, the goal of which is to stimulate commercial, political, or social obedience. Knowledge may be power, but information is not a priori powerful. And yet whether true or false, meat or fluff, smart or dumb, when information is presented in a designed context with the intent of drawing attention, it is given authority that it either deserves or not.

The designers represented in this section use various means to present complex information simply or complexly. Some are aesthetically striking, like the poster series for Ugly Mug Coffee (page 25), which uses discordant and variegated wood types in a particularly pleasing typographic composition to present wordy pitches on the efficacy of drinking java. Some are typographically dynamic, like the series of event posters for Nouveau Relax (page 32), which superimposes over photographs of everyday situations—fish market, subway station, streetscape—signs announcing art and culture activities.

Environmental super graphics are also a favored way of informing. The Eureka Tower car park garage (page 38) is a illusionary game, whereby key words—UP, DOWN, IN, OUT —are rendered at mammoth sizes in primary colors. But that's not all; from certain angles they are read perfectly, yet from others they are distorted to give the illusion they are posted in air. Another form of environmental graphic is not super but it is exceptional: for POEZIN (page 21), a veritable poster is made out of colored gaffing tape on a hurricane fence. This one-of-a-kind "rendering" is photographed for the final piece, but anyone seeing the original will doubtless be drawn in by its unconventionality. The POEZIN campaign also extends to painting information on human bodies and clothes in such a way as to grab the eye and not let go.

Along the same lines, mixing body art and taping messages to an environmental surface, the poster campaign for "Something Raw" for Theateer Frascati in Holland (page 17), is comprised of bodies and faces evocatively plastered with the event information using adhesive materials. The idea for presenting information on the human body started with tatooing, evolved into the less permanent sandwich board signs, and then in 1999 Stefan Sagmeister etched information for an AIGA lecture into his body with a razor blade, the bloody scabs became the lettering.

Information can be presented in a straightforward manner, like the poster "Osam Sati Rada, DVA Sata Pozorista" (page 31), though bold type and neutral graphic elements. The posters for Take One movie rental service (page 22), include a bold headline, like "You can have sex in a theater, but can you cuddle?" against a bright orange field. Or a more demonstrative typographic treatment draws attention.

Informing is tricky insofar as it is important not to overpower the information with conceptual cleverness or typographic conceit. This is way the advertisements for Nissan Shift (page 23) using custom street signs to promote its "free" GPS and air-conditioning is so smart. The signs, produced in the manner of European street markers suggest the alternatives to a/c: Heat Road, Humid Avenue, Sizzle Street, Sweaty Boulevard. In the most sublime way, these keywords trigger discomfort in the reader, forcing them to appreciate the value of free air-conditioning. Sure, many other car companies offer the same amenity, but this campaign gets under the skin.

Informing is the job of graphic design. Causing the receiver to act or alter behavior based on that information is the goal. But turning the information into truly useful knowledge is icing on the cake.

**03 EXCHANGE Atlanta—Braunschweig—Offenbach:
Buchkunst**
Client: Klingspor-Museum Offenbach
Designer: Uwe Loesch

Uwe Loesch shifts from abstraction to classic readability with
ease. This poster informs as it delights through its optical
playfulness.

Sensaway Typeface
Designer: Áron Jancsó
Photographer, Illustrator, Typographer: Áron Jancsó

Sensaway is an infinite contrast typeface designed for display
purposes. Dispersing the letterforms in this poster forces the
viewer to focus on the individual shapes.

Confluence

The Art Department at UNCG brings together four nationally and internationally recognized painters whose diverse approaches highlight the range of issues found in contemporary painting.

Margaret McCann, Lecia Dole-Recio, Julie Shapiro, Caleb Weintraub

In addition to the artists, prominent art critic and writer Dr. James Elkins will give a lecture, as well as moderate a panel discussion focusing on issues within painting today.

Sunday March 29, 2009
3:00–3:45 PM Lecia Dole-Recio, Falk Visiting Artist lecture, Weatherspoon Art Museum, Room 103
4:00–4:45 PM Dr. James Elkins lecture, Weatherspoon Art Museum, Room 103
5:30–7:30 PM Opening Reception, Maud Gatewood Studio Arts Building, Gatewood Gallery

Monday March 30, 2009
10:00–12:00 PM Panel Discussion. The four painters are moderated by Dr. James Elkins, Gatewood Gallery, Gatewood Studio Arts Building
4:00–5:45 PM Short lectures by Margaret McCann, Lecia Dole-Recio, Julie Shapiro, and Caleb Weintraub held at the Weatherspoon Art Museum, Room 103

3/29–3/31 2009

Tuesday March 31, 2009
12:00–2:00 PM Dr. James Elkins gives group critique of graduate students' work, Room 236, Gatewood Studio Arts Building

UNCG Confluence Symposium
Client: Barbara Campbell Thomas
Studio: Typografika
Art Director, Designer, Photographer: Erik Brandt

The layers of information on this poster illustrate the notion of confluence. The discordant types and bars of color area are both a mash-up and a logical means of directing the eye.

For a Green and Free Iran
Client: Green Bird/SocialDesignZine
Studio: Typografika
Art Director, Designer, Photographer: Erik Brandt

To commemorate Iran's Green Party, this is a joyful layering of information and party slogan. It engages those who advocate freedom and entertains those who enjoy a startling image.

June in Močvara, October in Močvara
Client: Club Močvara
Studio: Slobodan Alavanja
Art Director, Creative Director: Slobodan Alavanja

For these posters for programs at Club Močvara, the quilt of type and color is so aggressive that despite its cluttered appearance, it demands the viewer to stop and do.

5 x Berlin
Client: *Festival de l'affiche de Chaumont*
Studio: *Fons Hickmann m23*
Designers: *Fons Hickmann, Markus Büsges, Gesine Grotrian-Steinweg*
Photographer: *Nina Lüth*

The Festival de l'Affiche et des Arts in the French city of Chaumont is known as one of the most important graphic design festivals in all of Europe that presents a poster art exhibition. The theme in 2006 was Berlin's design scene, so Fons Hickmann was invited to design the festival poster, the accompanying book, and the exhibition.

Should I Stay or Should I Go
Client: *m23*
Studio: *Fons Hickmann m23*
Designer: *Fons Hickmann*
Photographer: *Simon Gallus*

This announcement for the new website, fonshickmann.com, gives the facts and nothing but the facts—and a forest of birches, too.

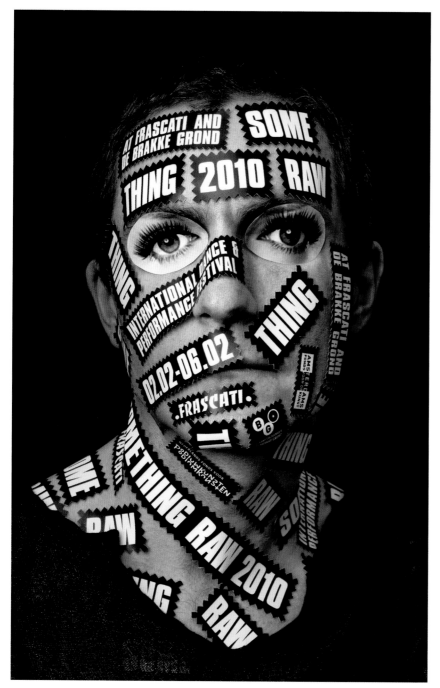

Something Raw
Studio: De Designpolitie
Photographer: Arjan Benning

The body is a depository of so much information. It is also a blank slate. This is a striking canvas on which so much can be applied in so many ways.

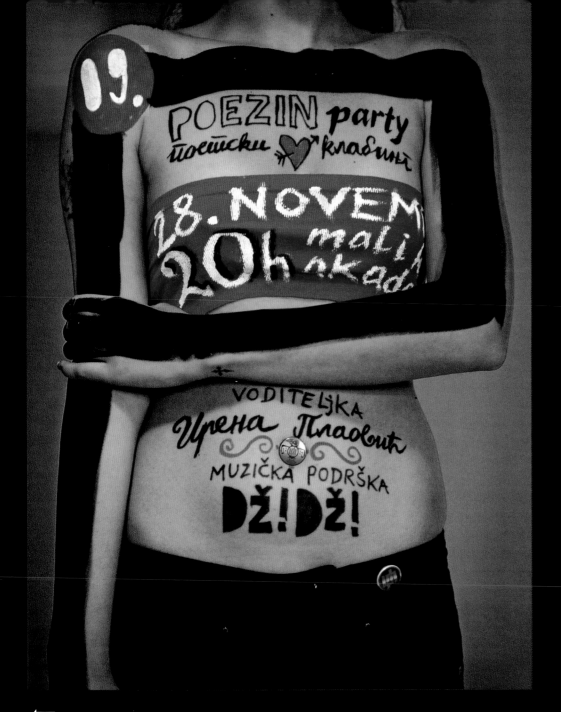

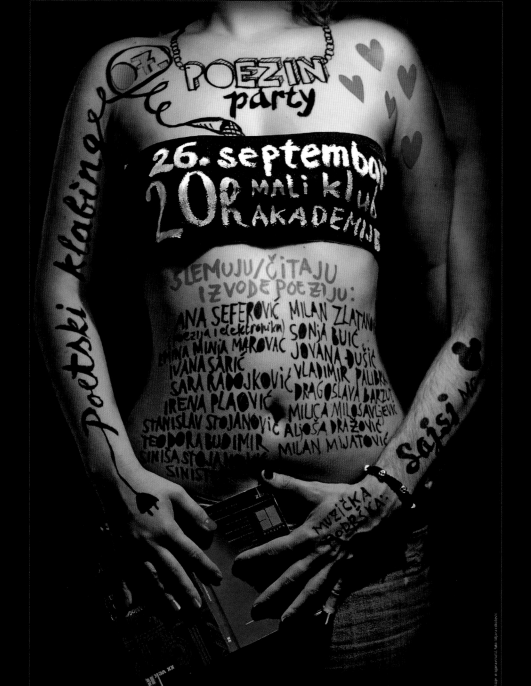

Poezin Posters
Client: Poezin
Art Director, Designer, Photographer:
Dragana Nikolić
Photographer (Poezin poster 07 and Poezin
poster 09): Biljana Rakočević

These posters were made for the
poetry event Poezin party (a.k.a. Poetic
clubbing). They were made as a combination of body-painting, handwritten
typography on bodies in different poses,
with a certain requisite. This poetry
event includes performance, slam, and all
kinds of engaged contemporary poetry.

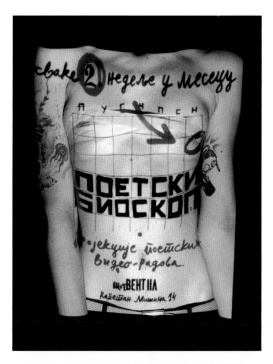

Poetski Bioskop (Poetic Cinema)
Client: *Poezin*
Art Director, Designer, Photographer: Dragana Nikolić

Three posters for the Poetic Cinema (Poetski Bioskop) were created by transferring
one drawing via video projector on three bodies. Poetic Cinema is a monthly event that
shows projections of short poetic films and videos.

Design, Money, and ...
Client: AIGA Dallas
Studio: Mirko Ilić Corp.
Designers: Mirko Ilić, Eytan Schiowitz
Art Director, Creative Director: Mirko Ilić
Photographer: Matthew Klein

This poster announced a lecture about the relationship between design, money, and politics. Because design is in a poor state, everything was made out of loose change.

Poezin XP
Client: Poezin, Belgrade, Serbia
Art Director, Designer, Photographer: Dragana Nikolić

Posters for the poetry event Poezin XP. This event includes performance, slam, and all kinds of engaged contemporary poetry. These are two of a series of open-air design posters done on wire fences all over the city with tape and felt pens. The surroundings and weather become part of the posters. And similarly to yellow police line tape, they mark a specific place—a special zone for poetry.

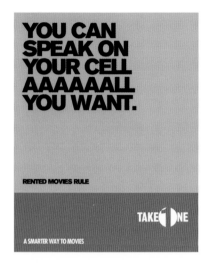

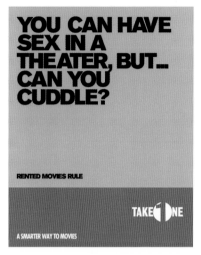

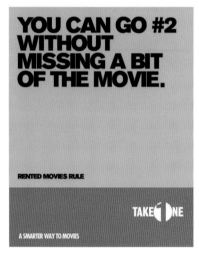

Cell, Cuddle, Date, #2, Pause, Undies
Client: Take One, Video Club
Studio: garcía+robles
Designer, Photographer: Victoralfredo Robles
Art Directors, Creative Directors: Oscar Rodríguez, Victoralfredo Robles

Facts can be communicated in various ways. The clever
quotations, in this otherwise staid campaign for a movie
rental service, hit the nail on the head.

Nissan, Heat Road, Humid Avenue, Sizzle Street, Sweaty Boulevard
Client: Nissan
Designer: Igor Miletic
Art Director: Tomislav Jurica Kačunić
Creative Director: Bruketa and Žinić OM/Moe Minkara
Photographer: Tomislav Jurica Kačunić
Copywriter: Daniel Vukovic

Using the street vernacular, in this case street signs, to convey messages about the Nissan automobile, is a means to inform and entertain.

Election Campaign: Jack Supports All Parties, Benevolent Dictatorships, The Other Kind of Socialist, Representative from Tennessee, Champagne, Common Ground

Client: Brown Forman/Jack Daniel's
Agency: Arnold Worldwide
Designer: Tim Mahoney
Art Directors, Creative Directors: Pete Favat, Wade Paschall, Wade Devers
Letterpress: Yee-Haw Industries
Copywriters: Gregg Nelson, Craig Johnson, Lawson Clarke

"Not too long ago, politics were simpler. Candidates believed in something, they stood by that belief, and that was that. And while these days it's a bit harder to find a politician with the courage to stand by their convictions," say the folks at Arnold Worldwide, "you know Jack Daniel's still does." With that said, by combining Jack Daniel's iconography and classic '50s and '60s American political design, and with the help of Yee-Haw Industries Letterpress, Arnold Worldwide created a series of authentic campaign posters and ads that got the Jack Daniel's message out there. "We covered the cities hosting the Republican and Democratic national conventions with wild postings, ran full-page newspaper ads and even set up Jack Daniel's Campaign Headquarters, in a bar of course, for all the thirsty supporters. Because if there's one thing we'll need when this is all over, it's a drink."

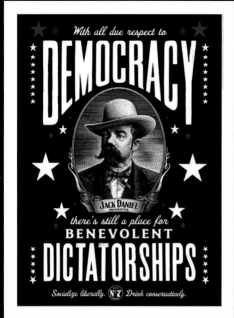

Ugly Mug Coffee

Client: Ugly Mug Coffee
Agency: Young & Laramore
Designer: Yee-Haw Industries
Art Director: Trevor Williams
Creative Director: Charlie Hopper
Copywriter: Bryan Judkins
Photographers: Harold Lee Miller, Gary Sparks

The Ugly Mug campaign is about maintaining high standards, but taking an unpretentious approach to do so. To give the brand a feel that communicated both unpretentious and premium coffee, Y&L partnered with traditional letterpress and design company Yee-Haw Industries. "We felt that the painstaking art of letterpress was key to creating a signature graphic tone," admit the Yee-Haw folks, "first and foremost because letterpress is both unpretentious and handcrafted. Ugly and beautiful."

Cubs Outdoor
Client: Chicago Cubs
Agency: Jones
Designer: Meng Yang
Creative Directors: Scott Maney, Dan Madole
Writer: Scott Maney

When provocative comments are made on billboards, the first instinct is to shunt them off as hyperbole. Perhaps these are. But in sports, hyperbole is part of the information fans receive every day.

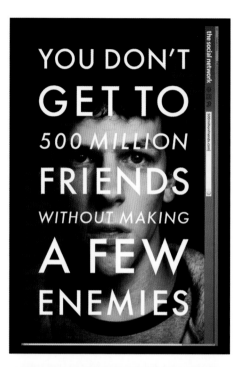

The Social Network
Client: Columbia Pictures, Sony
Agency: Kellerhouse Inc.
Designers: Neil Kellerhouse
Art Directors, Creative Directors: Neil Kellerhouse, David Fincher, Josh Goldstine
Copywriters: Neil Kellerhouse, John Blas
Photographer: Frank Ockenfels

Who really wants to see a movie about the founding of Facebook? At the time there were 250 million members, but why hadn't they made a film about Bill Gates, or the guys who started Google? As Neil Kellerhouse notes, "No big stars (Justin Timberlake is not box office gold, yet), boring title. So, why do I want to see this film? I think this poster had a big job to perform. That's why I like to call it an effective awareness device. It makes you want to know more."

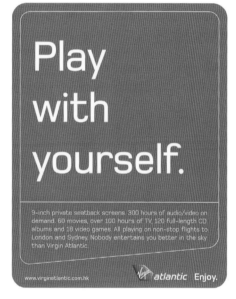

Play with Yourself
9 Inches of Pleasure
Client: Virgin Atlantic
Creative Director: Patrick Tom
Art Directors: Lorraine Liu, Patrick Tom
Copywriters: Dave Wong, Rico Poon, Chris Kyme
Illustrators: Karly Chan, Queenie Chan
Production Manager: Aliena Lai
Account Services: Adeline Chu, Peggy Chan

These advertisements use the venerable trope of innuendo and double entendre to get the message out on the extra legroom, and the eighteen video games, available on Virgin Atlantic.

Oblikobranje
Client: Designers Society of Slovenia
Studio: ZEK Crew
Designer: Tibor Kranjc
Art Director, Creative Director: ZEK Crew

The billboard project was created for
Oblikobranje Exhibition of the Designers
Society of Slovenia. A week before the
exhibition, the billboard was covered in
newspaper. On opening day, the word *oblikobranje* (meaning "formreading") was
discernible. By then the newspapers were
only covering the letters, as the rest had
been unveiled by weather and curious
passersby. Pasting the message on a billboard using newspaper pages is meant to
decompose or degrade after exposure to
the elements. It is also designed to make
the passersby take notice.

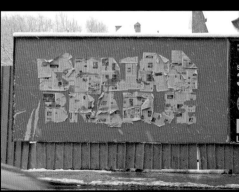

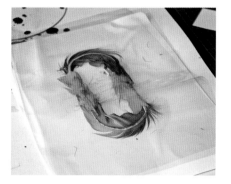

**William Fitzsimmons—
The Sparrow and the Crow Tour**
Client: SSC Group GmbH
Designers: Stefan Guzy, Björn Wiede

Singer-songwriter William Fitzsimmons handles the theme of his recent divorce on his album *The Sparrow and the Crow*. The designers took the idea of a fight between sparrow and crow—in which they would both be sure to lose a few feathers—literally, and created a typographic photogram out of numerous sparrow and crow feathers.

Revolution

Client: Theatre Atelje 212
Agency: Metaklinika, Belgrade
Designer: Nenad Trifunovic
Art Directors: Nenad Trifunovic, Lazar Bodroža,
Dušan Đorđević
Illustrator: Lazar Bodroža
Photographer: Dušan Đorđević

For the theater posters for *Revolution*, the visual
identity relies on left-wing aesthetics. Atmo-
sphere in the photographs, contrast relations of
black and white surfaces, and large typographic
printouts are reminiscent of political propaganda
materials. The graphic stylization reimposed itself as the basic element of the season's identity.

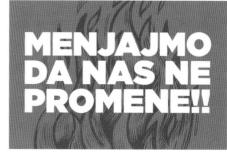

Relax vous Souhaite la Bienvenue
Client: Théâtre de Chaumont, Le Nouveau Relax
Designers: Anette Lenz, Vincent Perrottet

This is the first poster for a newly constructed theater in the small city of Chaumont in France. The building was converted from a cinema and bowling alley into a theater. The hand-drawn Relax type is fashioned after the old sign. The program was printed in a newspaper format—after the local newspaper had criticized the meaning of having a theater as addressing only to the intellectual elite of the city. So the designers' answer was the program in the form of the local newspaper; the poster became the front cover of the newspaper with doodles on it.

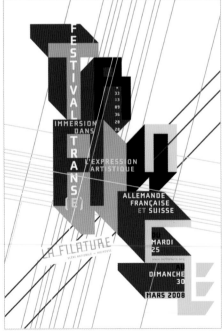

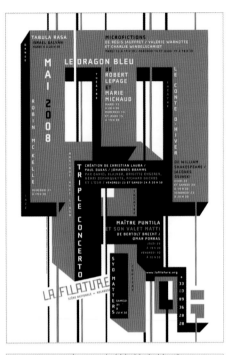

La Filature

Client: La Filature
Designer: Anette Lenz

Anette Lenz has the capacity to seamlessly fit a significant amount of data into an image without it seeming overwrought.

Secret of Art
Client: School of Visual Arts
Designers: Milton Glaser, Molly Watman
Art Director, Creative Director: Milton Glaser
Photographer: Matthew Klein

Art is both an illusion and a reality. This play on the secret wrapped into a ball suggests the temporal and physical essence of the spirit and the object.

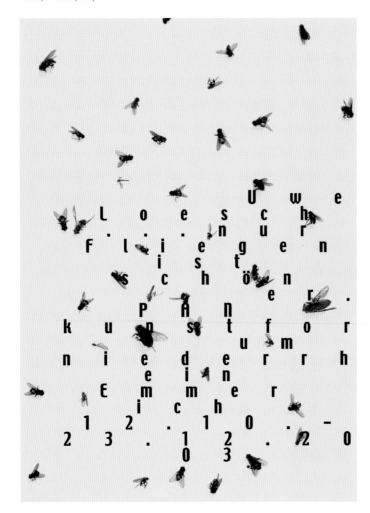

Uwe Loesch … nur Fliegen ist Schöner (Uwe Loesch … Fly by)
Client: PAN kunstforum niederrhein, Emmerich
Designer: Uwe Loesch

Illegibility has its charms. This poster for an appearance by poster designer Uwe Loesch is not fly-by-night, but it does have a temporal quality.

Ben Oyne, Photographer and Film Director
Client: University of Wuppertal
Designer: Uwe Loesch

One way to get information across is to use contrasts. This black-and-white poster uses positive and negative space to the best advantage, and does so without any image other than the snaking type.

Rendez-vous Chorégraphiques de Sceaux 2003
Client: Les Gémeaux/Sceaux/Scène Nationale
Art Director, Designer: Michel Bouvet
Photographer: Francis Laharrague

This poster was designed for an annual dance festival in the
theater Les Gémeaux, near Paris, with cutouts and string in such
a way that it's hard to ignore the craft involved.

Robert Klanten Lecture
Client: Pforzheim University, School of Design
Designer: Stefanie Schwarz

This poster for a lecture with the publisher Robert Klanten gives
a lot of information, but the conceit of designing books, putting
all its pages into a row, takes the onus off the excessive type.

Eureka Tower Carpark Wayfinding System, Melbourne
Client: emerystudio
Studio: emerystudio
Art Director, Designer: Axel Peemoeller

Signage is the *sine qua non* of information—simple and recognizable in an instant. The distorted letters align to the direction indicating words, *in*, *out*, *up*, and *down*, when standing at the right position.

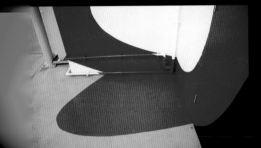

What if Switzerland wins the Euro08? Will these football fields see more action?

What if wheat prices keep rising? Will the restaurant here still sell spaghetti for only 12 francs?

What if our town has a budget surplus? Will they finally pay someone to cut this bush?

What if the Green Party gets into the Federal Council? Will they forbid these lit-up billboards?

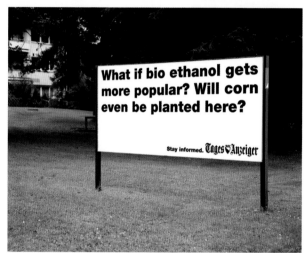

What if KPMG grows? Will the restaurant next door sell more lunches?

What if bio ethanol gets more popular? Will corn even be planted here?

What if everybody has a mobile phone? Will children have no idea what this thing to the right is?

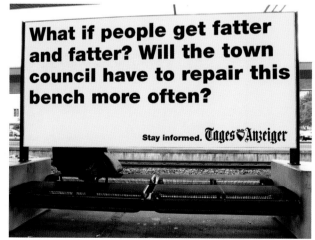

What if people get fatter and fatter? Will the town council have to repair this bench more often?

120 Individual Posters
Client: *Tages-Anzeiger*
Agency: Spillmann/Felser/Leo Burnett
Art Director: Katja Puccio
Copywriters: Peter Broennimann, Diana Rossi, Martin Arnold, Patrick Suter
Creative Directors: Martin Spillmann, Peter Broennimann

This campaign for Zurich's newspaper, *Tages-Anzeiger,* includes 120 individual billboards, each uniquely created for its specific location. These are both clever and curiously informative.

Manystuff Reflet

Client: Manystuff
Studio: Jean Jullien
Art Director, Designer, Photographer: Jean Jullien

This poster for the Reflet exhibition, organized by Charlotte Cheetham of Manystuff in 2008, in Toulouse, France, is like the medicine that tastes good. Lots of data presented in a delightful manner.

...THEN WE TAKE
BERLIN PART.2
11.01.–16.02.2008

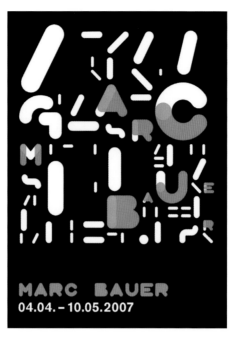

MARC BAUER
04.04.–10.05.2007

A.I.R. ONE
ARTISTS IN RESIDENCE
20.06.–26.07.2008

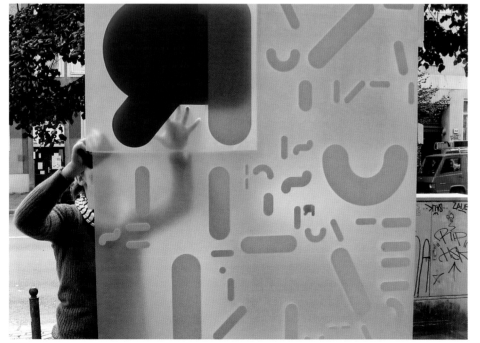

Substitut Berlin
Client: Substitut Contemporary Art Space
Studio: onlab, Berlin
Art Directors, Designers: Nicolas Bourquin,
Thibaud Tissot
Typographer: Thibaud Tissot

Substitut is a nonprofit exhibition space with
the aim to present Swiss artists in Berlin. The
name is composed of *subculture* and *institute*
and indicates its mixed nature. Onlab's main
principle for the corporate identity was to play
with typography in a non-Swiss way—free as
opposed to strict, and playful as opposed to
formal. The interior of the space is designed to
be unfinished with crude walls that reveal the
layers of the space's authentic past, hence the
typography was designed to be multilayered:
only when composed, the two typographic layers
reveal the content of the exhibition. This element
of decoding and unveiling suggests Substitut's
unfinished and emerging nature.

This Terrain Is a Joke: Goats, Snakes, Penguin
Client: Nissan Middle East
Agency: TBWA\RAAD, Dubai
Art Director: Daniel Djarmati
Copywriter: Sandeep Fernandes
Creative Director: Milos Ilić
Typographer: Daniel Djarmati
Illustrators: Radoslav Zilinsky,
Niklas Lundberg

The Nissan Xterra is so rugged,
it makes the toughest terrain
look like a big joke.

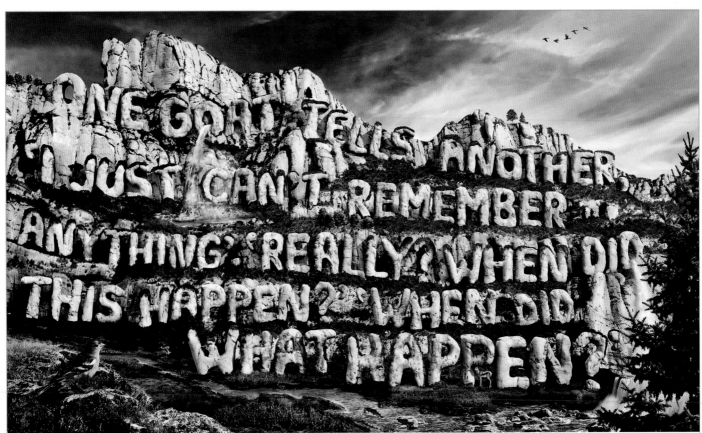

No terrain too serious. Nissan Xterra.

SHIFT_the way you move

History Rising

Designer: Amir Berbic

Cities aspire to develop iconic skylines that will carry them into the world of images and memorable postcards. The project "History Rising" is created from a collection of visual and verbal messages recorded from billboards in the city of Dubai. Slogans, such as "The Future of History Begins" and "We've Set Our Vision Higher," were used to promote the city's developments. Through change in material and shifts in scale, the ambitious catchphrases assume a different character. In this iteration of the project, the text is cut out from images in postcards of Dubai. The designer uses literal iconic flatness as a spatial metaphor. The flatness of the postcards and the superimposed slogans refer to the aspired meaning in the image of architecture.

Revolución

Client: Lizzie Design
Agency: La diez Publicidad, Uruguay
Art Directors, Designers: Pablo Alvarez, Guillermo Varela
Photographer, Illustrator, Typographer: Javier Venerio
Copywriter: Pablo Alvarez

These illustrated walls of type may seem like they should topple, but instead they provide a clear view of the information.

Days of Belgrade 2007

Client: City of Belgrade
Art Director, Creative Director: Slavisa Savic

Days of Belgrade is a four-day traditional cultural manifestation. Four giant Cyrillic letters for *DAYS* are placed in the main pedestrian street in city center. Each letter presents a day and also shows the theme of the program for that day. (*A* for *Art* ...) The letters are festival decoration, meeting points, info points, and gates. They are readable from both sides, and every letter has "two legs" so it does not close the street and obstruct the passage.

The Salvation Army

Studio: Hat-trick Design

The aim of the Salvation Army's new international headquarters building was to be seen as open and inclusive—*transparent* and *evangelical* were both key words. The architects created a very transparent building, where staff can be seen working in the glass rooms. The solution was to use transparent colored vinyl on glass, creating a stained-glass effect to reflect their evangelical nature. Light interacts with the signs throwing colored beams around the building, varying at different times of the day and year. The uplifting Bible quotations on the outside engage visitors and passersby, and again speak volumes about the organization's religious background. A small alteration to the *t* created an appropriate twist.

2

AGITATE

SUPPORT

PROTEST

ADVOCATE

The language of advocacy has a common goal: alter behavior and act upon instincts, whatever the outcome may be.

Designers create messages that rouse audiences to support, and therefore engage in, an issue or event, cause or mission—or anything else that falls under the rubric of advocacy. Doing so is a large challenge. How these messages are framed can mean the difference between action and inaction. Activating the conscience of an otherwise information-saturated segment of the population is not as easy as it sounds. Beautiful typography and elegant imagery are not always the most effective motivators. Pleasingly designed compositions may lull the viewer into acquiescence rather than spark the flame that steams the engine. The right balance of "good" and "appropriate" design is required, and this cannot be predetermined with a one-size-fits-all template. What pushes our buttons or not is situational and contextual. Behavior is not impacted by design alone; other environmental, emotional, and social factors contribute to whether a targeted message hits the mark.

Arguably, the most effective advocacy missives are the ones that use surprise—even shock—to draw attention and impart a command. "Help Hunger Disappear" (page 58), with the six-foot-tall word *hunger* made from stacked Campbell's soup cans, is a textbook example. Graphically it employs familiar labels, but the cumulative impact of seeing hundreds of cans forming the word hunger is surprising enough to demand more than a second look. The fact that the cans are meant to be removed, thus disassembling the word, provides an interactive component that most printed billboards or posters cannot achieve. It is surprising, commanding, and demanding all at once.

Not as cleverly designed but just as smartly conceived is the campaign titled "I'm Sorry. We Could Have Stopped Catastrophic Climate Change . . . We Didn't" (page 61), demanding action at the Copenhagen 2009 climate change conference that uses ironic prescience to move the masses. By aging the faces of today's world leaders—including Barack Obama and José Luis Zapatero—to appear as they might look in 2020, the campaign sets up the possibility that by not acting on climate change today, they made the planet worse off over a decade later. Apologies do not help, so the viewer is asked to "act now."

Although "I amsterdam" (page 56) is not political in tone or content, it is advocating for citizens to take ownership of their city. *I am* in red and *sterdam* in white as six-foot-plus-tall letters is as in-your-face as a statement can get with as minimal means as possible. The street installation advocates ownership while allowing for interactive play. The slogan "I amsterdam" is memorable and empowering.

Street objects as agitprop are effective advocacy tools. The "Make Trade Fair" (page 57) protest against the World Trade Organization uses the idea of equality among trading nations as its basic message but underpins the sentiment with messages emblazoned on colorful shipping containers that catch the eye and leave a mental "cookie." What says trade better than these ubiquitous containers.?

The "Climate Change" (page 52) campaign transforms everyday objects, flora, and fauna into letters that spell out the words in question. Rendered in a storybook representational drawing style, these posters are an interactive game that invites the audience to play and learn, while absorbing the message.

Change may be an amorphous thing to advocate for or against, but it is a charged word. It suggests a new beginning or it can be a tired bromide. When it is posted on the street to announce that "Victoria is Changing" (page 69), it implies the command that the people of Victoria should embrace whatever is to come. Or if cynical, it could mean "spare some change," but even that sentiment provokes a certain kind of behavior.

Possibly the most poignant example of advocacy is the send-up of the typical cardboard homeless sign—which has become such an urban streetscape fixture. For the "= Less Poverty" campaign (page 73), the ironic statement "Hungry. Will Work For Dignity, Respect, Human Rights" speaks to more than just a hot meal—to more than mere survival. In this vernacular scrawl, these words have powerful meaning that reminds everyone that there is more to life than just living.

The images and campaigns under the Advocacy umbrella demand attention. Designed to trigger response, passivity is not an option. Whether the design advocates social change or consumer engagement, the language of advocacy has a common goal: alter behavior and act upon instincts, whatever the outcome may be.

Mercat de les Flors
Client: Mercat de les Flors
Studio: toormix
Designer: toormix

Mercat de les Flors is a multidisciplinary space in Barcelona focused on dance and other scenic shows. Toormix created the identity based on the name (*flors* means "flower" in Catalan). The idea was to make a radioactive flower and play with very strong visuals with masks and broken graphics.

War and Peace
Client: Friedenshaus Berlin
Art Director, Designer, Typographer, Illustrator: Lex Drewinski

Lex Drewinski uses the opportunity of making theater posters to play with words and symbols. Each poster involves a word or symbol or both that sums up, with minimal means, the essence of the play or plot—or both at once.

Pause

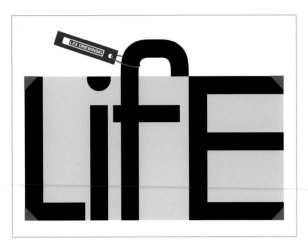

Life

Nostalgia

To Be or Not To Be

Money

Put in Prison!

Polish Airlines LOT

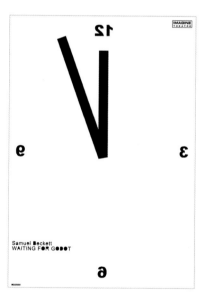

Waiting for Godot

Stop

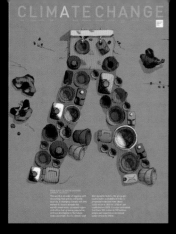

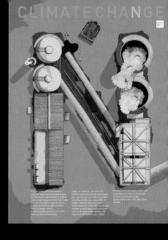

Posters for Climate Change Exhibition

Client: Centre for Media Studies (CMS), India

Studio: tiffinbox and doornumber3

Art Directors, Designers: Dwarka Nath Sinha, Rohit Chaudhary, Sriparna Ghosh

Transformation of objects into letterforms is a common conceit of designers. These speak to nature and climate, while advocating a smarter future.

Climate change is the crisis of this century. Temperatures and sea levels are rising, droughts and floods are increasing, water and food supplies are dwindling and each one of us will get affected. And we are responsible for the state the world is in today. We started it and we need to stop it. It requires bold change and it is all in our hands.

That is why CMS VATAVARAN, this year, is focusing on climate change. Because it is our today and tomorrow.

CONSIDER
COMMIT
COOL

A CMS Environment
Climate Campaign

The basic idea is that every individual can be kind of a "superhero" who can make changes and affect change on cultural and social progress in their own community, and take an active leading role in changing society. Posters are very noticeable, very effective, and suggestive—by choice of the specific stylization, colors, typography, and composition.

Amsterdam World Book Capital
Studio: KesselsKramer

Employing everyday, yet surprising, surfaces—
garbage bags, laundry, grass—to spell out its
message, KesselsKramer announces Amsterdam
as Book Capital in a very unbookish manner.

Experiment Amsterdam

Studio: KesselsKramer

Everyday photographic scenes paired with
surprising uses of type add to the dramatic
presentation of this curious message.

I Am Amsterdam
Strategy: Matthijs de Jongh
Art: Erik Kessels
Copywriters: Dave Bell, Lorenzo de Rita

Making a slogan into an interactive
sculpture on the street, the billboard
transcends its passive nature and
becomes a demonstrative means of
capturing attention.

Make Trade Fair
Client: Oxfam
Strategy: Matthijs de Jongh
Art: Erik Kessels
Copywriters: Dave Bell, Lorenzo de Rita

Combining the real cargo containers with
Oxfam's cautionary message forces the
brain to perceive reality and criticism as
a single piece of communication.

Hunger/Helping Hunger Disappear
Client: Campbell Soup Company
Agency: Leo Burnett Toronto
Creative Directors: Judy John, Israel Diaz
Art Director: Anthony Chelvanathan
Copywriter: Steve Persico

Using twelve thousand Campbell's soup cans, the designers spelled the word *hunger*. People were encouraged to remove a can from the display and donate it. The more people donated, the more the word and the problem of hunger disappeared. The campaign has been running for three years and continues to grow in the number of displays being built.

Operacija Grad (Operation City)

Client: Pravo na grad
Designer: Dejan Dragosavac Ruta

This is a series of banners reading, "The City Belongs to Everybody, Not Just to Them" and "Total Sellout." The demonstrators are suspending helium-filled letters spelling the word for quit.

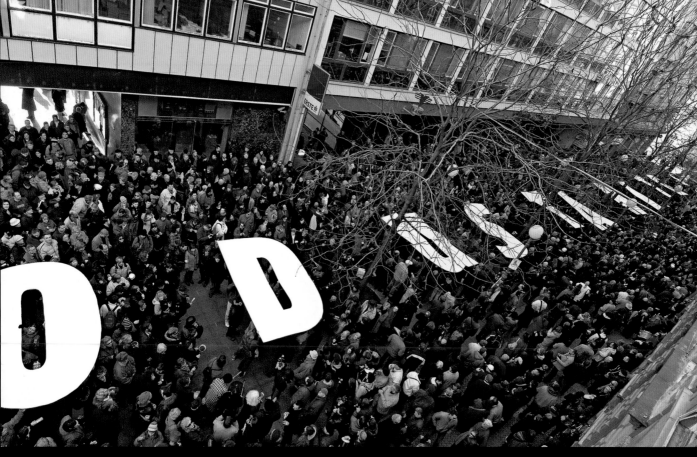

Apology from the Future
Client: Greenpeace International
Studio: Arc Communications
Art Director, Typographer: Toby Cotton
Copywriters: Toby Cotton/Greenpeace
Photo Researcher: Karen Guy
Photographer: Greenpeace/Christian Åslun

Using photo manipulation to project
world leaders twenty years into the
future, this poster campaign makes
an eerie commentary on the future
that very well might be.

LDP
Client: Liberalno Demokratska Partija
Art Director: Mirko Ilić
Designers: Mirko Ilić, Aleksandar Maćašev,
Nikola Andric, Jee-eun Lee

Mirko Ilić's stencil logo for the Liberal
Democratic Party of Serbia suggests the
immediacy of youth. The exclamation
point with the period below the baseline
is the mnemonic that emphasizes the
thrust of the identity.

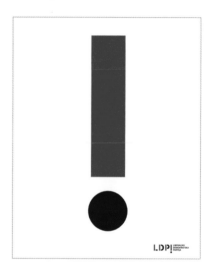

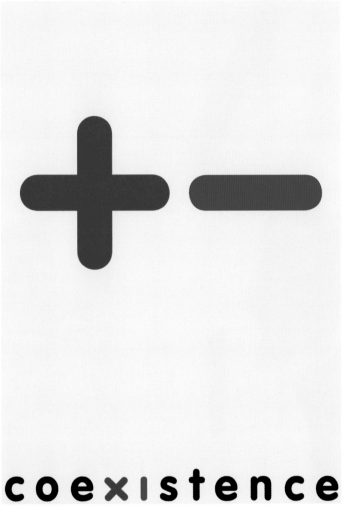

coexistence

Coexistence
Designer: Władysław Pluta

Władysław Pluta has created a sign/symbol that immediately refers to the idea of coexistence without resorting to cliché or stereotype.

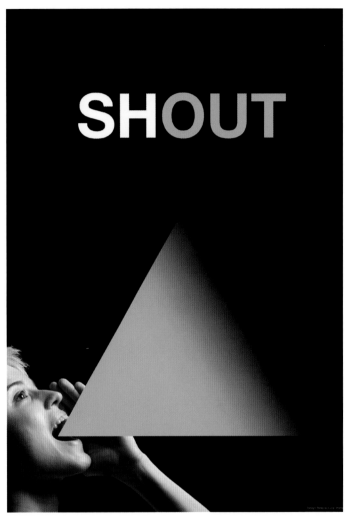

Shout
Art Director, Designer: Mirko Ilić
Photographer: Igor Mandić

Building a visual vocabulary from commonly known images and icons is the essence of graphic communication. Mirko Ilić uses the Rodchenko literacy poster together with the AIDS purple triangle—worn in the Nazi camps by homosexuals—to convey an AIDS prevention message.

Go with God

Client: Ermida de Nossa Senhora da Conceição
Studio: R2
Art Directors, Designers: Lizá Ramalho, Artur Rebelo
Photographer: Fernando Guerra

The Hermitage of Nossa Senhora da Conceição was built in Lisbon in 1707. Since reopening in 2008, this small chapel has been used as a gallery. One of the things that fascinated the designers was the chapel's original function as a place of worship. The dual presence of divinity and popular culture led them to play with idiomatic expressions in the Portuguese language that refer to God. This collection of popular expressions highlighted the diversity of words, proverbs, and idiomatic expressions. They used general expressions, such as "God is good and the Devil isn't so bad" or "God save us from the bad neighbors on our doorstep." The texts were read by passersby at different rhythms over the course of the day.

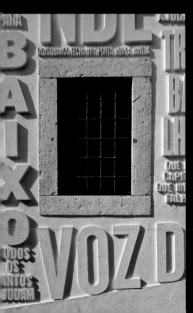

Story Vase (Blue)

The story on this vase: "I already made plans for the future. If I would get a life threatening illness, I have signed up for legal wise. This will give me legal advice, handicap coverage for my family, and a wheelchair if necessary. My dream was to get married and to own a motorcar."

Story Vase (Black)
Client: Editions in Craft
Designers: Front, Beauty Ndlovu (Siyazama Project)
Photographer, Illustrator, Typographer: Anna Lönnerstam

The Story Vases tell the personal stories of five South African women. Living in remote villages in KwaZulu-Natal, they are members of the Siyazama Project, a collective of women who work with traditional bead craft. Recorded by the Swedish design collective Front, the stories are the unique documentation of the daily life of women in rural, post-apartheid South Africa. They are stories that are rarely told and seldom heard. The story on this vase: "My name is Beauty. When I was young I dreamt of my own house. I used to draw houses, and I wanted to become a decorator. Now I have built my own house. I have three children, and I am happy. I have taught them how to make beads, so they can make their own income."

Atelier van Wageningen 3
Studio: Atelier van Wageningen
Art Director, Designer: Atelier van Wageningen

Employing nature to highlight this typographic/poetic/playground poster for promotion, the typeface *PURE* ensures memorability. In the Dutch language, *papier* means "paper."

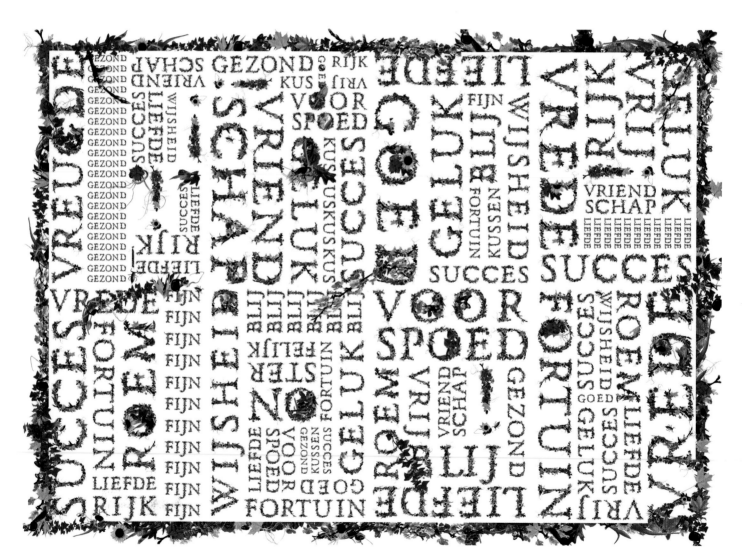

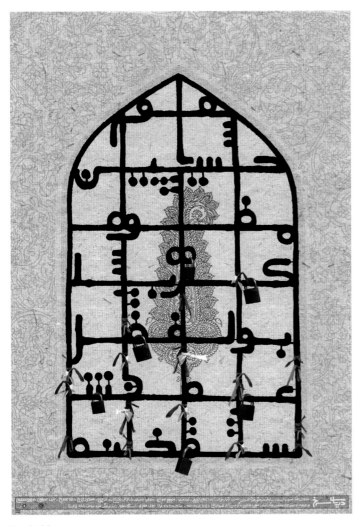

Saghakhane

Client: Tehran Municipality
Designer: Rashid Rahnama

Saghakane is a place to pray to God, for Emam Hosein. Designer Rashid
Rahnama shows the soul of Saghakane by using Persian typography and
the words *Emam Hosein, God, Thirsty, and Karbala*. The type, says Rahnama,
"is actually showing the shape of Saghakane."

Futuretainment Book
Client: Mike Walsh, Author of *Futuretainement*
Studio: Frost Design
Art Directors: Vince Frost, Quan Payne

The design element was particularly important to the theme of the book *Futuretainement*, which follows the consumer-led revolution in the media and entertainment industries. The graphic style is a pastiche of '50s modernist design. Vince Frost notes that "arrows are used throughout to emulate the forward movement of time, and the progression of the industries documented in the book."

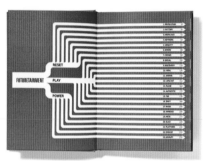

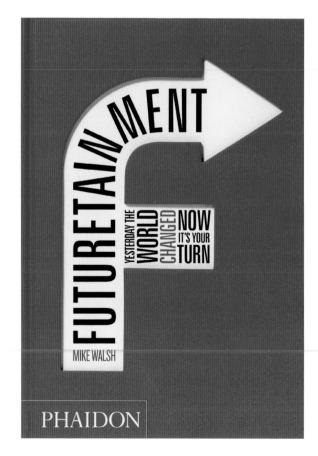

Victoria Is Changing

Creative Directors: David Kimpton,
Jim Sutherland
Designer: Alex Swatridge

A billboard site became available in
Palace Street, Victoria. The property
developer, Land Securities, has a large
number of schemes that will change the
area in the future. The brief was to utilize
the site to herald "Victoria is changing"
without going into specifics in advance
of future developments. Two thousand
recycled plastic windmills were screwed
onto a printed panel, spelling out the
word change. These constantly spun in
the strong winds in Palace Street and
provided a talking point for local businesses and residents.

**Good Design, Good Business Exhibition
Posters and Window Display**

Client: Lieu du Design, Paris (exhibition
from Museum Für Gestaltung, Zurich)
Studio: Helmo (Thomas Couderc,
Clément Vauchez)
Art Directors, Designers: Thomas Couderc,
Clément Vauchez
Silkscreen Printing: Lezard Graphique

Seen by passersby from the street, the
eyes in the center of these posters for an
exhibition about Swiss graphic design
avant-garde at Gaigy, in Lieu du Design
(Paris), act in a hypnotic, all-knowing
fashion.

Operacija Grad (Operation City)
Client: Pravo na grad
Designer: Dejan Dragosavac Ruta

This is a series of billboards inviting citizens to participate in the debate about the city, through the conference and art exhibitions. There are three questions on the billboards: Who owns the city? Privatization of the public. For whom? Who uses the city?

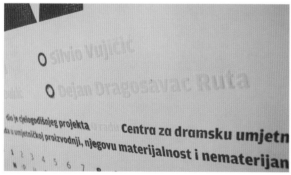

Ne/vidljivi Rad (In/visible Work)
Client: CDA (Centre for Drama Art)
Designer: Dejan Dragosavac Ruta
Author: Silvio Vujičić

This is part of the project about labor curated by Centre for Drama Art. It was realized as a series of artistic interventions and discussions on the issue of specific characters of the artistic production, its material and immaterial impact, managing, and labor costs.

I volti della Bosnia (The Bosnia Faces)
Designer: Leonardo Sonnoli
Client: The City of Pesaro Cultural Center

This poster, designed for a photographic exhibition about the war in Bosnia, utilizes a strong central image of a child playing on a burnt-out tank in front of a heavily beaten road sign to Sarajevo. The large letter *B*, overlaid on the image and reversed out of the road sign, dramatically draws the viewer's attention to the poster.

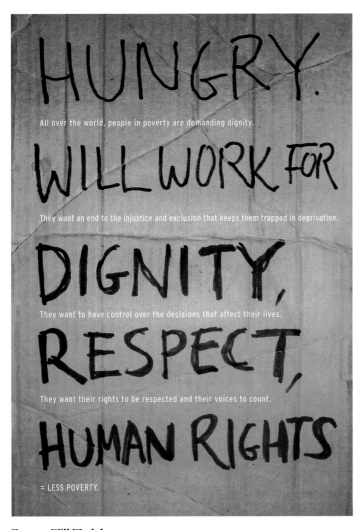

Hungry. Will Work for...
Client: Good 50×70
Studio: Jee-eun Lee
Art Director, Designer, Illustrator: Jee-eun Lee

This is an instance where handwrought lettering, the kind used by homeless persons, works a lot better to signal a strong message than more "official" typography.

Will Think for Salary
Studio: Roger Keynes
Art Director, Designer, Copywriter: Roger Keynes

As one of many Australian advertising creatives who were let go in May 2009 during the global financial crisis, Roger Keynes needed to get himself a job, an interview or, at the very least, noticed by the ad industry. Starting with the classic, "Will Think for Food" sign, he used the familiarity and topical nature of that graphic, but with a twist, "so it didn't undersell my creative value," he says. It worked. Keynes got calls from ad agency creative directors right away, and he is now busy consulting with four ad agencies.

Smoke Detectors
Client: Yellow Pages
Agency: Shalmor Avnon Amichay/
Y&R Interactive Tel Aviv
Chief Creative Officer: Gideon Amichay
Executive Creative Director: Tzur Golan
Creative Director: Amit Gal
Art Director: Ran Cory
Copywriter: Paul Paszkowski
Account Manager: Adam Avnon
Account Supervisor: Shiran Chen Barazani
Account Executive: Galia Ashri
Planning: Hilla Tamir, Zohar Reznik

Using various three-dimensional visual puns, these billboards for Israeli yellow pages touch the visceral as well as the visual parts of the brain.

Ironing

Tire Repair

Lawyers

Mirrors

Couples Therapy

Circumcisers

3

ENGAGE

tickle

ENJOY

PLAY

Play adds dimension to design, enabling the viewer to have more active participation in it.

Here's a fact everyone should know: design is play. Here's a command everyone should obey: designers must play!

Play is how we learn and teach others. "I use the term play," noted Paul Rand in *Graphic Wit* (1991), "but I mean coping with the problems of form and content, weighing relationships, establishing priorities." He went on to assert, "I don't think that play is done unwittingly. At any rate one doesn't dwell over whether it's play or something more serious—one just does it."

Rand's last declaration, "One just does it," is borne throughout this entire chapter. Not a single designer represented herein was ordered to play. However, each was faced with a problem that demanded solutions. Getting from problem to solution requires a methodology—whether it is tried and true or ad hoc, the common route begins with trial and error, which is the first step in the play-principle.

Don't confuse play with entertainment. Both are serious, but play is, for the most part, for oneself—for the muse—while entertainment is for others. Play comes first, entertainment comes second. Still, to entertain is to play. But to play is not always to entertain. Nonetheless, in this section, all the playful examples are designed to be seen, experienced, and appreciated by others. In this sense, they are indeed entertaining. Yet they are placed in this section because their primary function is revealing the degrees, levels, and stages of play at work.

What else by playful fancy is the word *home*, constructed in neon (page 80), or the word *style* (page 79) made from venetian blinds—what purpose do they serve other than a means of seeing how many different materials can be played with that result in letters? These are not the only experiments with form.

Play is not, however, exclusive to surprising materials — although surprise itself is endemic to play. For Guimarães Jazz '09 (page 91), the lettering announcing the acts follows the contours of the stand-up bass giving the impression the musician is both playing the lettering while conjuring it from his instrument. The transformation of one thing—lettering—into another—the essence of sound—is a playful conceit that forces the viewer to experience the otherwise two-dimensional design in many dimensions.

Play is also a transformation of one familiar thing or object into another. Hembakat Är Bäst (page 87) involves turning bread into the title of the cookbook. Similarly, an entire alphabet was made from laundry (page 87), including pants, shirts, and blouses. Going a playful few steps further, Wearable Typography (page 86), are twenty-six people wearing lime green shirts contorting their bodies to look like individual letters of the alphabet (both upper and lower case). Another example (page 86) that required a platoon of double-jointed people, is an alphabet made entirely from legs and feet—now that's a feat.

The most recognizable example of playful graphic design is not the contortionist's tricks but the more intellectually difficult parody of existing icons. DASH Courier Service advertising campaign (page 99), sending up more famous courier brands, is both playful and inspired. UPS becomes *OOPS*, FedEx becomes *FedExcess*, and Priority mail becomes *Priority Fail* (ouch!).

Twisting one thing into another is another essence of play. Another cover for *Metropoli* (page 89) transformatively parodies its own logo by making it from the pages of faux books.

In each case, the play adds dimension to the work, enabling the viewer to have more active participation in the work. Without the playful aspects of design, well, why bother?! "People who don't have a sense of humor," admonished Paul Rand, "really have serious problems."

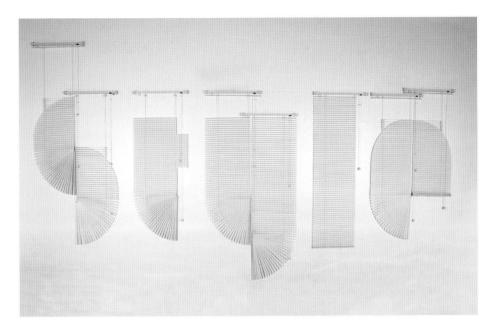

Venetian

Client: ELLE Decoration Magazine (UK)
Designer, Typographer: Andrew Byrom

Venetian is a stencil typeface design commissioned by *ELLE Decoration* magazine (UK). It was inspired by the forms created when opening and closing a venetian blind.

Interiors Light

Designer, Typographer: Andrew Byrom

The initial concept for Interiors Light was inspired by Marcel Breuer's Wassily Chair and was simply intended to be a rounded chrome tubular steel version of the original Interiors typeface design. The limitations of working in neon were tough on the original concept. The design was reworked several times and began to embrace the constraints of this beautiful and delicate material.

Byrom TSS

Designer, Typographer: Andrew Byrom

Byrom TSS is a "pop-up" temporary signage system. Each letter is fabricated from waterproof nylon wrapped around a fiberglass pole frame (similar to the construction of a modern dome tent). An elastic cord running inside the hollow poles allows the design to collapse into a small bag for storage. The design is intended for use in shops, galleries, conferences, and so on.

St. Julian 3-D

Designer, Typographer: Andrew Byrom

St. Julian is a 2-D/3-D blackletter stencil typeface. The wall-mounted 3-D version is constructed from steel. Its message comes in and out of recognition as the viewer moves past.

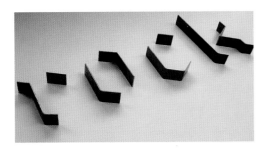

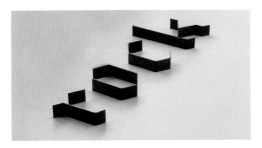

Interiors

Client: DHub de Barcelona
Designer, Typographer: Andrew Byrom

Interiors was originally conceived as a digital font and was inspired by an old wooden chair in the corner of Andrew Byrom's London office that, when looked at from a certain angle, resembled the letter h. Using the three-dimensional principles of this simple form, and closely adhering to type design conventions, twenty-six letters of the alphabet were drawn and generated as a font. They were later constructed in three dimensions using tubular steel into full-scale furniture frames. Because the underlying design concept is typographical, the end result becomes almost freestyle furniture design. Letters such as *m, n, o, b,* and *h* can be viewed as simple tables and chairs, but other letters, such as *e, g, a, s, t, v, x,* and *z,* become beautiful abstract pieces of furniture. The design is shown here in use in a logo celebrating the opening of DHub de Barcelona.

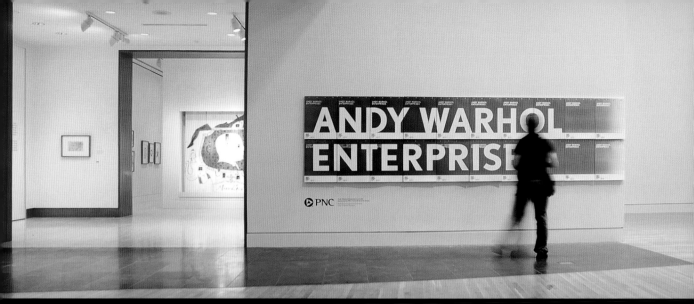

Andy Warhol Enterprises
Client: Indianapolis Museum of Art
Studio: Indianapolis Museum of Art
Designer: Matt Kelm
Art Director: David Russick
Additional Credits: Printed by Faulkenberg
Printing Co./Exhibition curated by Sarah Green
and Allison Unruh

This is the title graphic for "Andy Warhol
Enterprises," an exhibition curated by
Sarah Green and Allison Unruh, explor-
ing the commercial component of Andy
Warhol's work. For the title graphic, the
designers wanted to explore a format that
referenced formal aspects of Warhol's
art including repetition, vibrant colors,
and a tight grid. The solution they created, made up of four thousand posters
and combined into twenty pads, also
provided a unique opportunity for visitors to take a part of the experience home
with them. "Andy Warhol relied a great
deal on repetition in his work, and helped
to democratize art by 'mass producing'
much of his work in his Silver Factory,"
Matt Kelm adds.

Still Life Comes Alive
Creative Director: Kyosuke Nishida
Art Directors: Kyosuke Nishida, Brian Li Sui Fong, Sean Yendrys
Designers: Kyosuke Nishida, Brian Li Sui Fong, Sean Yendrys, Dominic Liu, Stefan Spec, Duc Tran

This is a life-size typographical installation using thousands of pieces of paper folded and glued together to form the sentence that describes and illustrates the concept.

Rock 'n' Roll, 2007
Designer: Helmo

This exhibition in Fondation Cartier pour l'Art Contemporain
(Paris) is a chronological fresco (150 x 4 m) about the rock 'n'
roll movement.
©Helmo

Letterform for the Ephemeral

Art Director, Designer: Amandine Alessandra

The letterform Amandine Alessandra was trying to define had to be flexible enough to keep the message relevant and up to date as its context changed, while having the visual presence of a giant billboard. "This led me to experiment with wearable typography. As a single person can mimic a whole set of letters, the message can change, from one movement to another," Alessandra says. The idea of using clothing (fluorescent green) as the basis for a legible alphabet is play. Making quotation marks by waving arms, is play gone wild.

Body Type

Art Director, Designer: Amandine Alessandra

The Body Type alphabet is an experiment on possible organic letterforms emerging when reframing the body.

The Personal Alphabet
Art Director, Designer: Dunja Pantic

Who would have imagined that everyday laundry could become a typographic toy? That is the beauty of play. Dunja Pantic uses jeans, shirts, and laundry tote bags to make a colorful twenty-six letters.

Hembakat är bäst (Homemade Is Best)
Client: IKEA
Agency: Forsman & Bodenfors
Art Directors: Christoffer Persson, Staffan Lamm
Copywriter: Fredrik Jansson
Photographer: Carl Kleiner/Agent Bauer
Stylist: Evelina Bratell

This cookbook cover uses metamorphically playful letterforms, which are not only legible but edible—especially tasty are the ümlauts.

Los Miserables

Client: Unidad Editorial Revistas SLU
Art Director, Designer: Rodrigo Sánchez

With a walnut shell for the *O* and woolen fabric for the E in *Metropoli*, the only thing that trumps it for temerity is the apple core in *Miserables*.

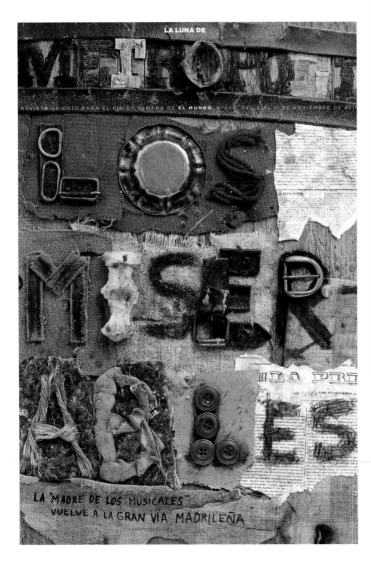

Iron Man II

Client: Unidad Editorial Revistas SLU
Art Director, Designer: Rodrigo Sánchez
Photographer: José María Presas
Illustrator, Typographer: Lucía Martín

For a story in *Metropoli* about the *Iron Man* sequel, the lettering is obsessively composed of ironworks. The parentheses take the prize.

Librerías Raras
Client: Unidad Editorial Revistas SLU
Art Director, Designer: Rodrigo Sánchez
Photographer: Ángel Becerril
Typographers: Ricardo Martínez, Rodrigo Sánchez

There is no better way to promote a special book issue of *Metropoli* than to draw all the type by hand on the page-side of a number of books.

Telemetropoli
Client: Unidad Editorial Revistas SLU
Art Director, Designer: Rodrigo Sánchez

This issue of the magazine is about the delivery services in Madrid. On the cover appears all the best services available. The nameplate for this occasion is playfully changed from *Metropoli* to *Telemetropoli*, and the bigger title on the page features the phone number of the Metropoli's newsroom secretary.

Armageddon
Client: Unidad Editorial Revistas SLU
Art Director, Designer: Rodrigo Sánchez

Playing with optics focuses the viewers' attention on the decisive word on this cover of *Metropoli*— and upsets the equilibrium, too.

Guimarães Jazz
Client: Centro Cultural Vila Flor
Studio: Atelier Martino&Jaña
Designers: João Martino, Alejandra Jaña, Oscar Maia, Álvaro Martino, Filipe Cerqueira
Art Directors, Creative Directors: João Martino, Alejandra Jaña

To promote the 2009 edition of Guimarães Jazz, one of Portugal's major jazz events, a strategy was conceived to emphasize the spontaneity of this specific genre. All pieces of information are put in motion by the musician's flying fingers and the instrument's swinging strings, reinforcing the curvy shapes through the absence of color.

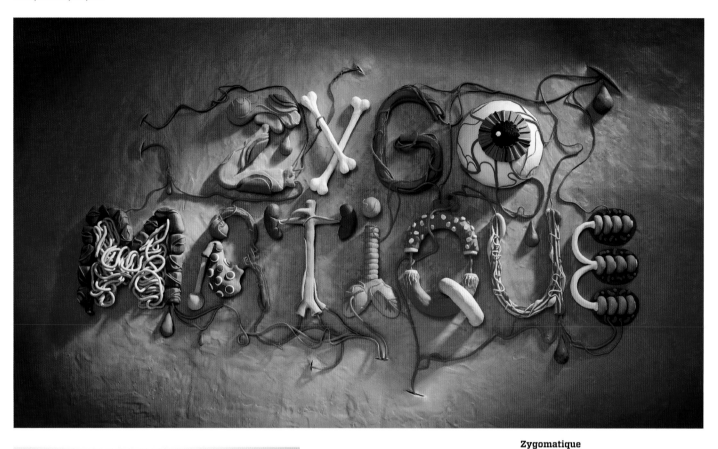

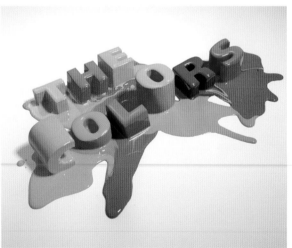

Zygomatique

Studio: Serial Cut™
Designer: Julien Brisson
Photographer: Paloma Rincón

Zygomatique is the French word for the *zygoma bone*, which is the head. The designer created this word with human body parts made of modeling clay.

The Colors

Client: Jotun
Studio: Serial Cut™
Photographer: Paloma Rincón

Real paint letters for the promotional image for the paint company Jotun look good enough to eat.

icon
Client: Serial Cut
Studio: Serial Cut™
Designer: Kristian Touborg
Photographer: Paloma Rincón

Made of Japanese candies, icon is a homage to the emojis, the icons that we all use in our smartphones for chatting.

ideal
Client: Serial Cut
Studio: Serial Cut™
Photographer: Paloma Rincón

The word *ideal* has universally positive connotations. Displayed here in a multicolor wire, it serves as promotion of Serial Cut's new update.

Isometrically Unexpected
Client: Serial Cut
Studio: Serial Cut™

Based on the block type signature of the Japanese designer Igarashi from the '80s, this composition pays homage to one of the most respected and visionary designers of the contemporary scene.

Series of CD Covers
Client: Radio France
Art Director, Designer, Photographer: Michal Batory

Letters are made from wax drips, water droplets, bird feathers, and glass shards—these are clever visual puns that give character to the meaning of the words and phrases in this series.

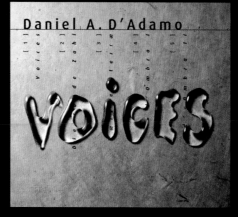

Kleid im Kontext (Clothing in Context)
Client: Gewerbemuseum Winterthur, tuchinform Winterthur
Studio: David Clavadetscher– Grafik Designer FH
Designer: David Clavadetscher

Fashion can be playful, seductive, and expressive; it excludes and includes, but it also represents a constant interplay between clothing and body, stillness and movement, the individual and the environment. The "Kleid im Kontext" exhibition centers on the performative aspect of dressing. The social context is explored, as is the connection between bodily awareness and the sense of living in the present. Some thirty Swiss fashion designers have been invited to create clothing compositions for this exhibition. Their works express a variety of approaches and moods that are independent of seasonal rhythms and conventional rules.

Blue Notes Typeface
Art Director, Designer, Typographer:
Agnieszka Mielczarek-Orzylowski

This typeface design was happily inspired by jazz of the great Billie Holiday.

Our Times by A. N. Wilson
Client: Picador
Designer: Alex Camlin
Art Director: Henry Sene Yee

For a book that traces the changes in British identity over the latter half of the twentieth century, "I chose to mix elements from two icons of design," Alex Camlin says, "the 1939 Ministry of Information 'Keep Calm' poster, and Jamie Reid's cover for the Sex Pistols' 'God Save the Queen' single, that serve as graphic 'bookends' for the era covered."

Exit Ghost
Publisher/Client: Houghton Mifflin Harcourt
Design Firm: Milton Glaser Incorporated
Designers: Milton Glaser, Molly Watman
Art Director, Creative Director: Milton Glaser

"The word *Exit* as seen inside a movie theater, manages to shed its light on the word Ghost. It is an exercise on metaphysics," says Milton Glaser.

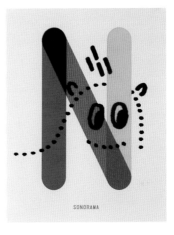

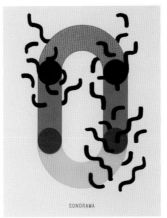

Sonorama 09
Client: Sonorama 2009
Designer: Helmo

For this art, sound, and music festival, "sound landscape" in the city of Besançon (France), the multiple overlays of color not only draw in the eye but pique the ears.

Poster Design Melchior Imboden

Designer: Melchior Imboden

Imboden uses color transparency and overprinting to engage, confound, and hypnotize through a soothing pattern.

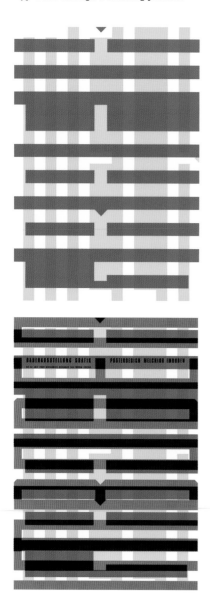

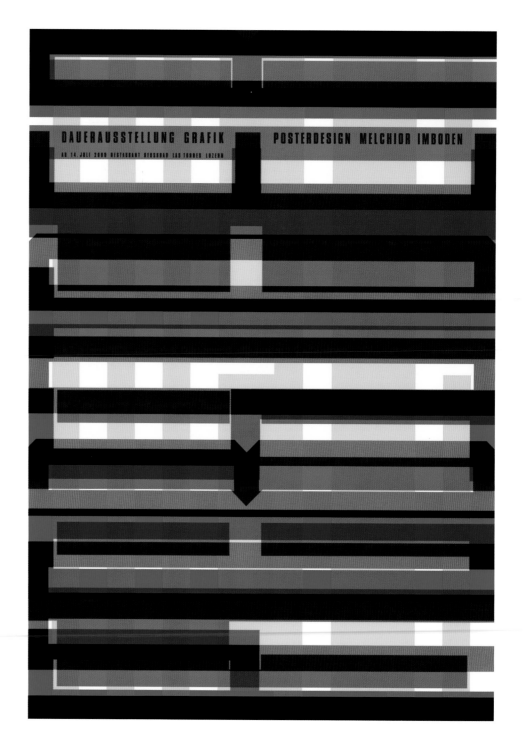

Carolinas' Most Reliable Same Day Delivery Service DASH—FedExcess, Oops, Sol, Priority Fail

Studio: Marked for Trade
Creative Director, Art Director: Phil Jones
Copywriter: Ryan Coleman

Parody is sometimes the most sincere form of flattery. Other times it is an effective tool for ridicule. Somewhere in between, Marked for Trade remixes the logos of the leading courier services to show that play can undercut his client's competition.

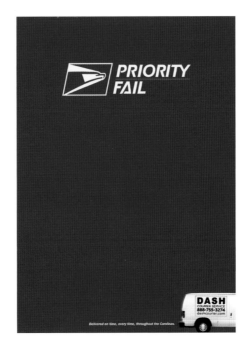

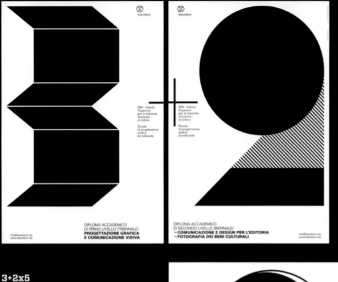

3+2x5

Client: ISIA
Designer: Leonardo Sonnoli

This series of posters, printed front and back, shows different 3s and 2s, in reference to the three years it takes to get a bachelor's degree, plus two years for a master's degree. The posters were designed to hang with 3 and 2 side by side.

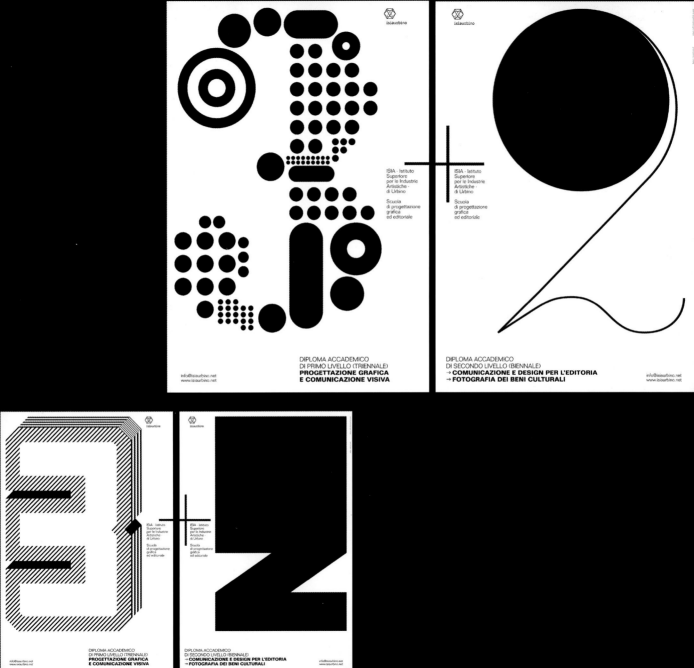

4

BEWARE

FOREWARN

OBEY

CAUTION

Cautionary messages force the receiver to go somewhere or do something to avoid dangerous consequences.

This is an old but insightful joke: Two dimwitted (or maybe just stoned) hunters were walking through the woods when they found a sign that read, "Bear Left." So they went home!

Analyzing the joke seriously for a moment, one could argue that the sign cautioned them *not* to hunt a dangerous bear—and since she left anyway, they acceded and saved their miserable hides. But, as the joke actually indicates, they stupidly misread the sign and departed. Apologies for killing the joke through overanalysis, but this tale provides us with an object lesson, of sorts.

Bear with me. Directional signs are not routinely cautionary. But cautionary signs sometimes indicate directions, as in "Danger, don't go there." Cautionary messages force the receiver to go somewhere or do something to avoid dangerous consequences. The design of caution is essential to safety.

One could argue, however, that *advocate* and *caution* are two sides of the same coin. To caution is indeed to demand action, which implies advocacy, which means a forceful message. But cautionary graphic design is differently nuanced. Advocacy is *support*, whereas caution is *beware*.

The language of caution also requires different idioms depending on the message, but always a similar forceful tone. In advocacy the "soft sell" is possible. Not so with cautionary missives. Barbara Kruger's "Don't Force It" (page 106), which is ambiguous enough to have multiple implications, must be forceful. Her "All Violence Is the Illustration of a Pathetic Stereotype" (page 105) will stop the viewer through the violent use of her Futura typography. To caution often means to shock.

There are many ways of cautioning and many things to caution about. "STOP AIDS" (page 109) is a simple enough typographic message that plays with the layering of letters and color. It advocates AIDS prevention and cure, but more definitively it cautions against being vulnerable to the killer disease. *Stop AIDS* means "safe sex." Even more hard-fisted is the visual pun using a common traffic sign with the word AIDS replacing STOP (page 108). Without having to say the word, the message is crystal clear.

A more subtle play on words (page 113) involves a familiar line of Shakespeare—"To be, or not to be?"—whereby the word war is ghosted behind the or. It cautions that the world can "be," but with war it will "not to be." The message is both overt and subtle insofar as the meaning is clear to any clear thinker, but also something of a stretch to pull Shakespeare out of the air. The rejection of any typographic flourish, however, forces the viewer to focus on the double entendre and not the design per se.

The latest grotesque photographs mandated by U.S. law to be used on cigarette packages (above the brand) are more effectively cautionary than many graphically designed posters. But that does not negate the heartfelt attempts by designers to alter behavior—especially among teenagers—to reject smoking. "Smile Now! Cry Later! Smoking Kills!" (page 111) relies excessively on "cool" typography. But the message is difficult to ignore. The idea that the payback on tobacco smoking will lead invariably to a miserable end is the kicker of this image. Nothing subtle about it.

Similarly, "Drugs Drag You Down—Till You're Under the Ground" (page 111) might have been executed with less horsey type and clichéd zombie illustration, but for the audience who "reads" this style, the message is decidedly appropriate. The only way to caution against the danger of drug abuse is through angry and shocking design.

The double take, a form of subtlety, is operative with the "Franco" image (page 108). Francisco Franco was the Spanish dictator from 1939 to 1975 who imposed a Fascist police state. It takes that understanding to appreciate the design of this cautionary poster. The typography is built on marching, fascist saluting people following in lockstep. At a distance, the image is unassuming. Up close it is a startling indictment specifically against Franco, yet also cautioning against the evils of the totalitarian cult of personality.

Another message against lockstep conformity is the cautionary one against anger (page 115), employing increasingly larger balloons to suggest the relative explosive power of assertive, angry, mad, and hostile behavior. Although the surreal image demands interpretation, once the message is perceived it forcefully shows how these volatile emotions can wreak havoc.

One of the most economical yet persuasive cautionary images in this section is "Fall" (page 116), with its three-dimensional letters tilting over. It both illustrates the word in a literal manner and cautions against the harmful impact of a fall.

Designing caution does not have to follow any particular format, but it does have to be clear enough so that when the viewer sees it there is no ambiguity. Of course, even the clearest signs can be misinterpreted, like the confused hunters who "went home."

All Violence...Stereotype
Designer: Barbara Kruger

Installation view, "Barbara Kruger"
exhibition, Mary Boone Gallery,
New York, 1991

Every 12 seconds a woman is beaten in the U.S.

25% of the violent crime in America is wife assault.

4 women are killed everyday by their husbands or partners.

60% of battered women are beaten while they are pregnant

DON'T DIE FOR LOVE

STOP

DOMESTIC VIOLENCE

Don't Die for Love
Designer: Barbara Kruger

Billboard for Liz Claiborne, Inc. Women's Work Project on Domestic Violence in San Francisco, 1991

Don't force it

Don't Force It
Designer: Barbara Kruger
Art Director: Steven Heller
New York Times Book Review cover

Barbara Kruger has not shied away from the grand public statement. Using her modern design palette of red and black with bold Futura type, and large-scale scoldingly cautionary phrases, she grabs the heart as well as the eye.

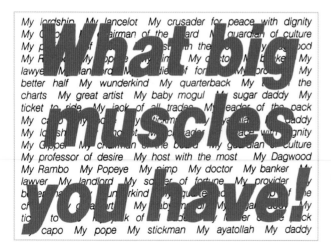

What big muscles you have!

What Big Muscles You Have
Designer: Barbara Kruger

Don't Be a Jerk
Designer: Barbara Kruger

Billboard, Melbourne, Australia, 1996

Help!
Designer: Barbara Kruger

Bus shelter project for Public Art Fund,
Inc., Queens, New York

Get Out
Designer: Barbara Kruger

Billboard for Liz Claiborne, Inc. Women's Work Project on
Domestic Violence in San Francisco, 1991

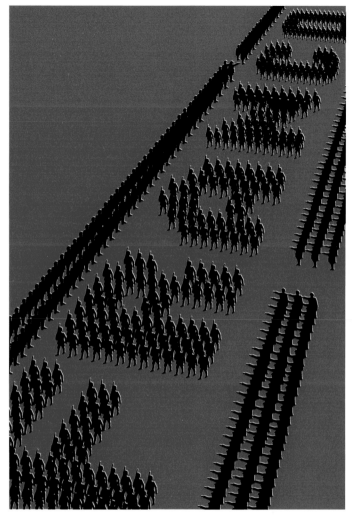

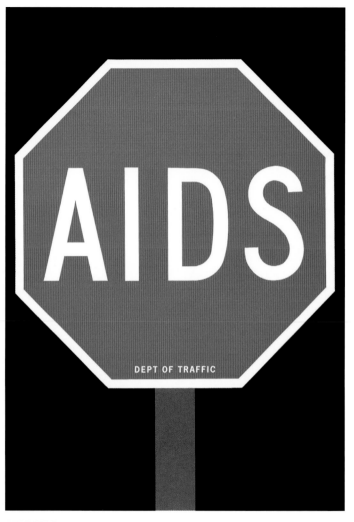

Baetulona
Client: Brrothers
Designer: Patrycja Zywert

This was an initiative by Brrothers, which invited one hundred designers and studios to take part in celebrating the history of Badalona city. The designer's brief was to illustrate the arrival of Spanish dictator Franco's troops to Badalona in January 1939, which was the beginning of Franco's regime. "I decided on a simple idea of creating a typographic image of marching soldiers forming the name of the dictator," Patrycja Zywert explained.

STOP AIDS
Art Director, Designer: Steff Geissbuhler

What says stop better than the familiar and ubiquitous sign? It is as recognizable as our own names. *AIDS* is a word that implies *stop* as well.

STOP AIDS
Client: ANTIAIDS Ukraine
Studio: Sommese Design
Art Director, Designer: Lanny Sommese

Lanny Sommese uses bold letterforms (and black and red, like Kruger) to typographically demonstrate the word *AIDS* being halted, taken over by the word *STOP*. The type in these three treatments serves as both word and illustration.

NOW Magazine

Client: *NOW* Magazine
Studio: Smith Roberts Creative Communications
Creative Directors: Malcolm Roberts, Arthur Shah
Art Director, Designer: Greg Kouts
Copywriters: Matt Hubbard, Brian Smith

While not cautionary in the strictest sense, these ersatz street stencils have the visual impact of a cautionary or advocacy image. Employing stencil lettering in this impromptu manner gives the impression that *NOW* magazine is truly of the moment.

Paragon—Anti-Drugs
Client: Paragon Marketing Communications
Studio: Paragon Marketing Communications
Art Director, Designer: Louai Alsfahani

This concept is rooted in the idea that drugs drag you down until you are under the ground.

Paragon—Smoking Kills
Client: Paragon Marketing Communications
Studio: Paragon Marketing Communications
Art Director, Designer: Louai Alsfahani

Similar to the Anti-Drugs campaign, this concept, using a twist on the cliché of a skull, is meant to caution and turn the viewer off to any hint of cigarette smoking.

Darfur
Client: Paradoxy Products
Studio: Mirko Ilić Corp.
Designer: Mirko Ilić, Daniel Young
Art Director, Creative Director: Mirko Ilić

This poster is about the genocide in Darfur, and is compared to the Holocaust, which happened during World War II. *DARFUR* becomes an acronym for names of different concentration camps during World War II.

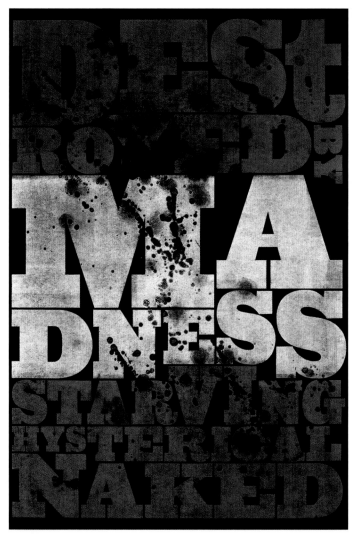

Madness
Studio: Daddy
Art Director, Designer: Bjørn Ortmann

This is part of a series of woodcuts inspired by the writings and life of the Beat Generation. But it also serves as a caution against insanity in favor of behavioral moderation.

To Be War/Or Not To Be
Designer: Mieczyslaw Wasilewski

The famous Shakespeare line, "To be, or not to be?" is cleverly transformed through this shadow technique. It asks the question whether it is nobler in the mind to have war or be at peace.

... And Our World Is Still Alive

Art Director, Designer: Tahamtan Aminian
Copywriter: Farshid Shahidi

Drawing attention to cautionary messages requires the marshaling of design and illustration in clever and eye-catching mannerisms, such as these by Tahamtan Aminian featuring the words "pain," "grief," "torture," "disgust," "prostitution," "isolation," and "persecution," as ashes (left) and an Iranian proverb (right).

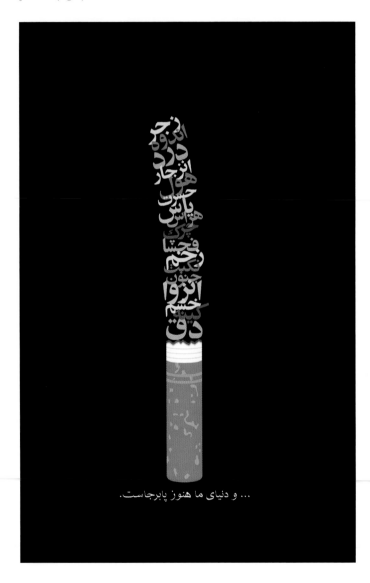

Visualizing Anger
Designer: Petar Pavov

Cautioning against anger is like blowing smoke into the wind. Which is why the more surreal manner of addressing the theme focuses attention on what anger does to an individual persona. It blows the head up and skewers the skin with unpleasant sensations.

"Ants," "Fall," and "Hole"
Designer: Petar Pavov

The visual pun used in this three-dimensional manner is a powerful tool for giving an otherwise simple message more resonance.

Forbidden Signs
Client: Sjef Meijman
Studio: EGBG - Martijn Engelbregt
Art Director, Designer:
EGBG - Martijn Engelbregt

Martijn Engelbregt entrenched himself for a week in a big nature park in Veenhuizen. The specific scenery inspired him to paint signs on recycled wood he found in the environment.

Broadcast Order Form
Client: VPRO
Studio: EGBG - Martijn Engelbregt
Designer, Art Director, Creative Director: EGBG - Martijn Engelbregt

Graphic design as data management: Martijn Engelbregt is an information-collecting fanatic. He puts a face to a method of dealing with information and the over-the-top nuttiness of it all normally overlooked by most designers. The dead-end questionnaire is his favorite element.

Yes, I Fill in This Coupon
Studio: EGBG - Martijn Engelbregt
Designer: EGBG - Martijn Engelbregt
Art Director, Creative Director: EGBG - Martijn Engelbregt
Photographer, Illustrator, Typographer: EGBG - Martijn Engelbregt

This form is a parody of the annoying coupons people have to navigate every day.

announcement to send in

counterscript

start asking immediately after first question is asked

telemarketer does not cooperate

if you get in a difficult conversation, make use of the conversation moves below and then continue with the script on the left side of the page

to **whom** am I speaking ? | could you spell your name for me please?

could you tell me how you found this phone number?

ooh, this way

and is this your full time job? ▷ part time | what else do you do for living?

full time | I am a houseman/-wife | I study | I have another job

ah nice, what do you study? | ah nice, what exactly?

that's funny, my neighbour does the same thing!

do you also live in ... ? (add your place of residence)?

incredible! | yes | no, in

and how long have you been in the telemarketing business? | oh, that's nice as well!

that's not very long | 0-5 months | 5 > months

$/€/£ per hr/day/wk/mnth

and, do you like your job? | that's quite long

$/ € /£ per conversation

no | yes | no clear opinion

that doesn't sound bad at all!

I think I would like this kind of job as well

do you get time off for going to a dentist?

why are you doing it then? | how much do you earn?

yes | no

is it important to have good teeth for your job?

yes | no

thank you for your information. would you mind giving me your phone number in case I need additional information?

which toothpaste would you recommend?

thank you and have a pleasant day. good bye

impression	+	+/-	-			+	+/-	-
accent				tempo				
word choice				volume				
enthusiasm				sympathy				

after finishing the conversation, cross-check these blanks to give an overall impression of your telemarketer

hang up the phone

your name

your street and number

your postal code

your place

your country

your phone number

send the counterscript to | fax the counterscript to | e-mail the counterscript to

EGBG Data Control Group
Schapenlaan 7a
1862 PW Bergen
the Netherlands

0031 · 20 · 620 95 73

martijn@egbg.nl

---

telemarketer refuses to provide information

Mr/Ms ... why don't you want to answer my question?

no time | other reason

when can I call you back? | date

hang the phone | have a pleasant day | time

continue with the script at the next conversation

telemarketer wants to know why you are asking questions

I would like to know more about the person I am speaking to right now Mr/Ms ... why don't we get back to my question?

telemarketer wants to know what happens to his/her answers

I can appreciate your hesitation Mr/Ms ..., however, this is an important piece of information used for verification purposes and I will handle it with strict confidentiality. With that in mind, would you consider and provide me with the information?

telemarketer keeps asking questions

▷ I can not answer your question(s) in interest of this investigation

▷ I can't provide this information because I need unprejudiced answers

▷ an answer to this question might jeopardise the partiality of this investigation and it would prove unreliable

▷ I am sorry, the information you ask for is unfortunately not available for you

telemarketer gets upset

▷ I can appreciate your concern, but aren't you calling me?

▷ don't you like talking with me?

▷ do you have a problem answering questions to a stranger on the telephone about which you don't know the purpose?

legend | titles for different parts

► follow the arrow

important instructions

▷ make the triangle of your choice black

text you speak

fill in the blanks when possible

difficult conversation moves

possible reactions of the telemarketer

questions about you

Anti-Telemarketing Counterscript
Studio: EGBG - Martijn Engelbregt
Designer, Art Director: EGBG - Martijn Engelbregt
Photographer, Illustrator, Typographer: EGBG - Martijn Engelbregt

Are you bothered by teleresearchers and telemarketers? Here is an opportunity to reverse the roles and ask the questions yourself. The direct marketing sector regards the telephone as one of its most successful tools. However, consumers experience telemarketing differently: more than 92 percent of consumers feel that commercial telephone calls are a violation of their privacy. Telemarketers make use of a telescript—a guideline for telephone conversations. This script creates an imbalance in the conversation between the marketer and the consumer.

Can You Answer This?
Client: IDFA, Docs Online
Studio: EGBG - Martijn Engelbregt
Designer, Creative Director: EGBG -
Martijn Engelbregt
Photographer, Illustrator, Typographer:
EGBG - Martijn Engelbregt

This is a flyer for an installation about
interactive documentaries produced on
recycled wood the designer found in the
environment.

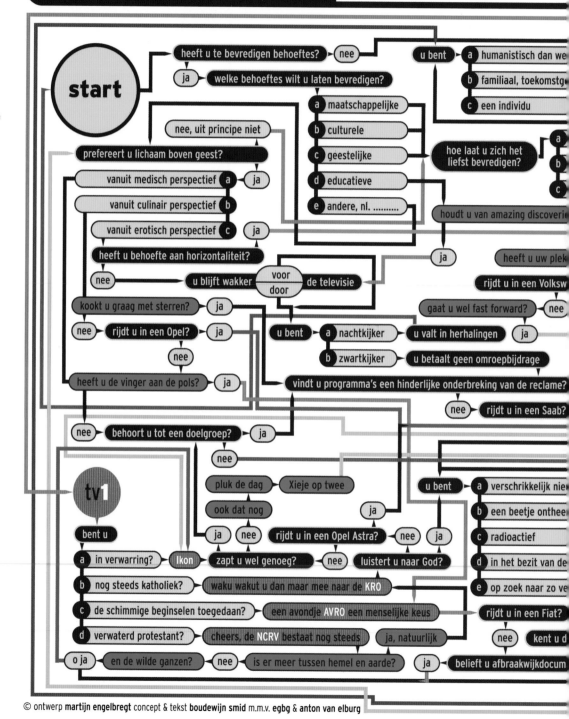

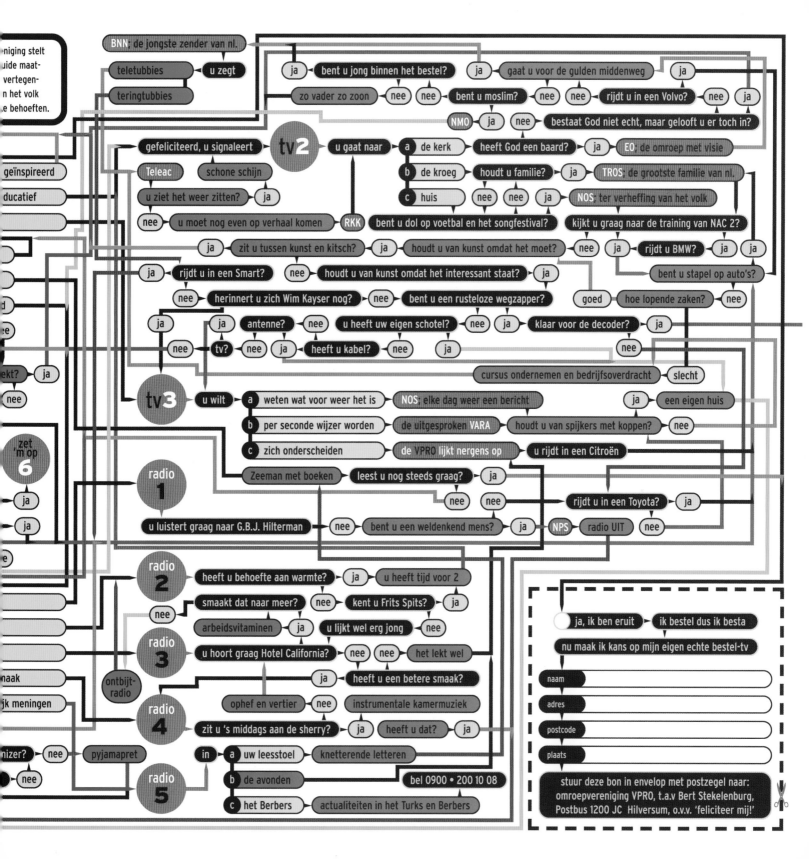

Please Touch

Client: MOT (Museum of Contemporary Art Tokyo)
Studio: EGBG - Martijn Engelbregt
Art Director, Designer: EGBG - Martijn Engelbregt

This three-dimensional form is a commentary on how people visiting the museum are being investigated while making choices. The route of each visitor was secretly registered and archived.

Revelations O.G.
Client: Street Canvas
Studio: EGBG - Martijn Engelbregt
Art Director, Designer: EGBG -
Martijn Engelbregt

Martijn Engelbregt made several walks from de Oude Groenmarkt (O.G.) in Dutch town Haarlem. Every day he chose a different direction. During the walks he devised new commandment signs, notices, warnings, and other signs, which he designated a specific place at specific locations.

One Moment of Patience Please
Client: Kunstpaleis
Studio: EGBG - Martijn Engelbregt
Art Director, Designer: EGBG - Martijn Engelbregt

Patience is a virtue, they say. This is an installation in the lobby of a former theater.

Will Be Retrieved Tomorrow
Client: Kunsteyssen
Studio: EGBG - Martijn Engelbregt
Art Director, Designer: EGBG - Martijn Engelbregt
Photographer, Illustrator, Typographer: EGBG - Martijn Engelbregt

This handpainted type on a large temporary art building situated in the middle of cheap furniture and interior shops, resembling the low value of the goods we surround ourselves with.

Zonde (Sin/Waste)

Client: Municipality of Utrecht
Studio: EGBG - Martijn Engelbregt

In Dutch there is one word for both *sin* and *waste*, so waste can be seen as the major sin of it all. For the municipality of Dutch city Utrecht, Martijn Engelbregt did this specific city marketing project. He also handed out 777,777 stickers with the word *ZONDE* throughout the city.

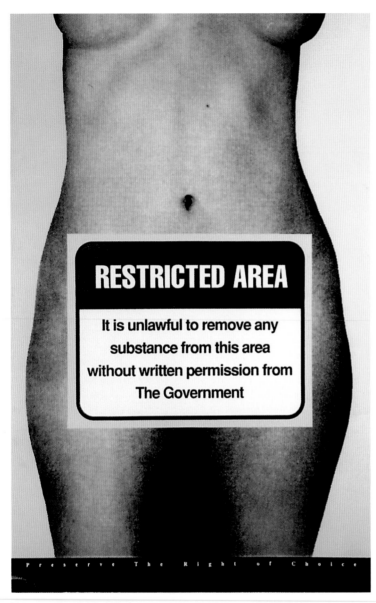

Preserve the Right of Choice
Client: Trudy Cole-Zielanski Design
Studio: TLC Design
Art Director, Designer: Trudy L. Cole

The poster attacks the absurdity of anyone (e.g., church or government) making decisions about a woman's body, other than herself.

Innerstate
Studio: Studio AND
Art Director, Designer, Typographer:
Jean-Benoit Levy
Additional Credits: Cafepress.com

A personal interpretation of the U.S. road signs system cautions the user that current signs are dangerous to the health.

Curb Your God
Client: Paradoxy Products
Designer: Daniel Young

A T-shirt with a terse admonition against
religious violence, using the plain vernacular
of public signage

Corporation
Client: Paradoxy Products
Designer: Daniel Young

Beware of anything that combines the
rights of a human with the money, motives,
and immortality of a corporation.

5

STIMULATE

ENLIVEN

EXCITE

ENTERTAIN

Much graphic design cannot afford neutrality; it must grab attention in crowded environments.

Always leave 'em laughing—a lyric in a 1903 song by Tin Pan Alley great George M. Cohan—is the unofficial mantra of stand-up comedians everywhere. It might be appropriate for graphic designers, too—as well as always leave 'em thinking . . . remembering . . . and doing! A large amount of graphic design is straightforward or neutral—"The facts and nothing but the facts, ma'am." But much graphic design cannot afford neutrality; it must grab attention in crowded environments and implant the seed (whatever it may be). That is exactly when the graphic designer must call upon various talents—one of which is to be an entertainer. Through wit and humor (or the graphic design equivalent of song and dance) the receiver is lulled into embracing the message. Entertainment is not just showbiz—it is design biz.

Entertainment and play certainly overlap. However, to entertain implies acting for an audience, while play suggests entertaining oneself. Paul Rand said that play is the most integral part of the design process. "Without play, there would be no Picasso," he wrote in *Graphic Wit* (1991). "Without play, there is no experimentation. Experimentation is the quest for answers."

It may not be an experiment, but what could be more entertaining—ergo memorable—than the series of posters for Amtrak (page 132), where torso and full-body drawings of everyday commuters have locomotives grafted to their heads. If a client heard the idea, they'd probably think the designer was "loco," which happens to be one of the campaign's headlines. But to look at these surreal images and read the demonstrative headlines (typeset in a version of Railroad Gothic—what else?) is an "aha" visual, as natural for the theme of "Trainiacs," as any more straightfoward image—and thrice as memorable.

Likewise, the oddball "Be Stupid" (page 134) campaign for Diesel clothes uses truly goofy and equally surreal situations (accompanied by provocative headlines) that can't help but entertainingly draw attention. Who wouldn't at least stop to look at a sexy girl standing at the side of the road with a traffic cone covering her head? Or a bikini-clad beauty photographing her own genitals while a lion (yes, a lion) looks on in the background? While the stupid theme is an enigma, it is an entertaining one.

A poster campaign for PNet, a job portal (page 131), asks "Tired of Office Politics" in a banner under a clenched fist, designed in the manner of Shepard Fairey. Above this in the series are simple yet demonstrative headlines, including "The Feminist. The Guy Who Hugs You A Little Too Long," which is engaging for its wit and truth.

Headline declarations can be pedantic, but when handled with tongue in cheek will have resonance. "Go to Hell vetica" (page 137) may not be very profound, but at a time when the Helvetica typeface has come back into vogue, it is a clever way of commenting on its fiftieth anniversary. It is also a perceptual game that demands the viewer decipher the joke. It may not take a long time to uncover the "reveal" but just long enough to entertain.

Speaking of games and puzzles, poster announcements for Jazz in Willisau (page 142), each a typographic optical challenge, forces the viewer to spend even more time than the "hell vetica" poster deciphering the message. One poster, "Bass Drum Bone," involves imbedding the message within colored dots that are almost impossible to read when close-up—but when at a distance it is totally clear. Another, "Die Rote Bereich," is a cascade of variously hued red lines, which is difficult to read even from a distance, but fun to attempt to do so. And another, with lettering composed of thin lines in white and yellow against black, is totally incomprehensible—yet hypnotic. Whether they do the job of conveying a message or not, the viewer cannot help but spend time trying to figure it out.

Messages for entertaining things—plays, films, books—are often entertaining as a tease. The "Fucking A" (page 141) poster for the New York Public Theater, which uses a similar hide-and-reveal lettering technique as the Jazz posters, also plays on the play's taboo title, which is only slightly obscured, making it easy to decipher. Although cursing is no more outrageous than not cursing, in American puritanical society, such words are not polite on advertisements. Therefore, the playwright and producer knew this would be a hard play to promote and review, so the poster is a means of announcing and provoking.

Revelation is both intellectually stimulating and entertaining. It forces the mind to make surprising connections, which very likely stimulate some chemical in the brain that makes one satisfied and thereby happy. For the Witness project, which uses video to be witness to otherwise secret or hidden events and acts, promotes itself with a poster titled "Making Truth Visible" (page 150), where the word *Truth* seems to simply (and without typographic fanfare) emerge from the cropped words *Making* and *Visible*. In the sense that the designer has invited the viewer into the conceptual process, this is an entertaining typographic exercise.

Connectivity occurs whenever the audience feels it is involved on some level with the design process. A good example of these are the British poster stamps (page 147) commemorating the Royal Shakespeare Company's fiftieth anniversary. Each stamp is a black-and-white photo from a performance of *King Lear*, *Romeo and Juliet*, and other classics, with raw hand-lettering scrawled around the characters. In the corner is, of course, the ubiquitous silhouette of the queen. The stamps serve multiple purposes aside from their main function. They provide icons for the plays represented. And because the lettering is so raw, they suggest informality. Shakespeare frightens some people—too olde English, and all that—but the informal type makes Willie more democratic.

Entertainment is one of design's functions. How it is accomplished, as the work in this section shows, is up to the designer's aesthetics, conceptual skill, and instinct for what best appeals to her audience.

PNet Office Politics Camapaign
Executive Creative Director: James Daniels
Art Director: Romy Lunz
Copywriter: Sarah Keevy
Typographers: Romy Lunz, James Daniels

For a job portal it is important to earn the user's confidence. Yet one way to do that is through graphics that speak to self-confidence. And it doesn't hurt to add a bit of irony, too.

Connections Are Made
Go Loco
Trainiacs Unite
Client: Amtrak
Agency: COLLINS: and The Martin Agency
Designers: John Moon, Mickey Pangilinan
Art Directors: Ty Harper, Raymond McKinney
Typographer: Chester Jenkins, Village

Among hobbyists, historians, and travelers, trains have a loyal following. These self-espoused rail fans are a passionate but niche community. Amtrak wanted to make their love contagious. So COLLINS: created National Train Day, a nationwide celebration of all things relating to trains. "We wanted rail fans to be our evangelists," explains Brian Collins. "We also wanted to celebrate their passion in a way that would be intriguing and inspiring to the general public. The "Trainiac" was born. Spanning a century of styling—his head a vintage steam engine and his wardrobe and body language more modern and relatable—Trainiac is the everyman who just happens to harbor this fanaticism for trains." The type is as big and powerful as the train itself: 600 point Linotype Alternate Gothic Condensed caps, and one of the biggest, baddest, fattest cuts of Futura, Monotype Extra Bold. Like the mood, the color palette is bold and simple.

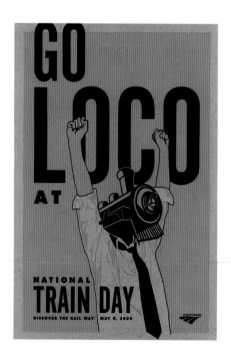

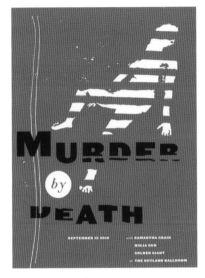

Murder by Death
Client: The Outland
Studio: Daniel Zender
Art Director, Designer: Daniel Zender

Clean typography is employed to contrast with the loose ink illustration. It also goes further by illustrating the illusion that the viewer is peeking through blinds at an innocent subject.

Frühlings Erwachen (Spring's Awakening)
Client: Jugendtheater Sempach
Studio: Erich Brechbühl [Mixer]
Designer: Erich Brechbühl

This is a theater poster for a play based on Frank Wedekind's classic novel, *Spring's Awakening*. Although difficult to read, when deciphered the result is quite entertaining.

Be Stupid—Diesel
Client: Riccardo Bellini
Executive Creative Director: Mike Byrne
Creative Director, Design: Kevin Lyons
Creative Director, Digital: Mat Jerrett
Art Directors: Ian Toombs, Coral Garvey
Print Production: Chris Whalley
Brand Strategy: Paul Graham
Communications Strategy: Geoff Gray
Digital Planning: Paul Graham, Alfred Malmros
Digital Production: Jon Shanks
Interactive Music Video Production: Stink Digital

At first the concept of "be stupid" seems counterintuitive when trying to sell a brand. Yet when paired with the ironic and quixotic visuals in these advertisements, the theme has a positive connotation. Stupid is not dumb; it is fun.

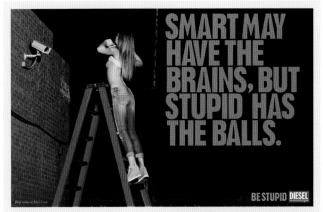

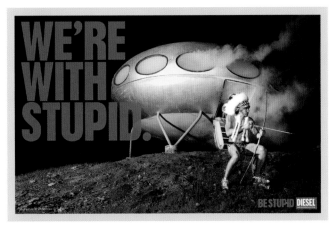

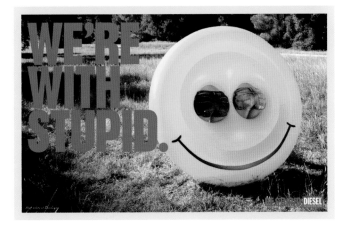

Crash
Studio: HK Reklamebyra
Art Director: Stian Ward Bugten
Copy Writer: Nina Bjørlo
Photographer: Arild Juul

This is part of a nightclub opening campaign with the Crash nightclub sign, joyously created with colored neon bulbs to attract the eye like moths to a flame.

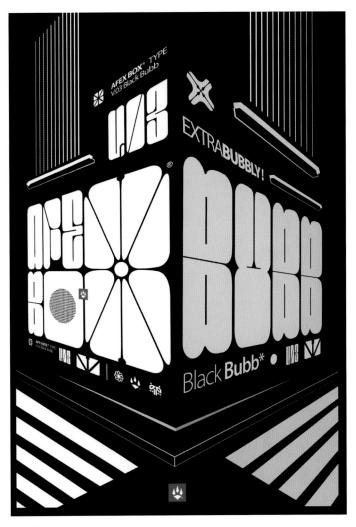

Go to Hell vetica
Client: Centre for Contemporary Art Ujazdowski Castle, Warsaw
Studio: Fontarte
Art Directors, Designers: Artur Frankowski, Magdalena Frankowski

Designers are often entertained by anything having to do with type and typography. And because of its serious demeanor, Helvetica is one of those faces that is quite easy to parody.

Afex Box Type
Studio: FX3™
Designer: Julien Gionis/KRFX

Afex Box is an experimental "Block Buster" fat display font. Inspired by top-to-bottom block graffiti letters, this display type is trying to invade as much space as possible.

Pirulí, Pirulón, Pirulero
Client: In collaboration with *étapes* magazine
Studio: David Torrents
Art Director, Designer: David Torrents
Photographer: Silvia Míguez

The poster, says David Torrents, "in Barcelona is almost dead. I made an action in order to change this situation." This carnivalesque poster, which states that very sentiment, was distributed in Barcelona on December 2010. The poster also was the cover of *étapes* magazine.

Xinacittà
Client: APQR
Studio: David Torrents
Art Director, Designer: David Torrents

The color-crazy graphics for the
Animation Film Festival of Barcelona
is virtually animated. The eye is drawn
into the patterns of hue. And the designer
avoided showing any one particular
animation in the process.

MILTON THEATRE

MILTON THEATRE PRESENTS
MACBETH

DIRECTED BY COLIN GRAHAM
DESIGNER ARTHUR MACARTHUR
PRODUCER ALFRED LEEDING
LIGHTING BRIAN ARMSTRONG
CAST INCLUDES
DICK RAND
JUNE PEARCE
JANE WATERMAN

ESMÉ MACARTHUR
STAN TURNER
NORMAN SLATER
KEN WILLIAMS
REG DUFF
BOB DAVIES
CHARLES SEARING
JO MILNER

9 SEPTEMBER - 8 OCTOBER
BOX OFFICE
0145388 2380

Macbeth Poster

Client: Milton Theatre
Studio: Lippa Pearce
Art Director, Designer: Harry Pearce

What is *Macbeth* in essence but a story about deception
and murder? Using the blood as a frame for the title of
the play is an entertainingly clever visual pun that both
illustrates and names the protagonist.

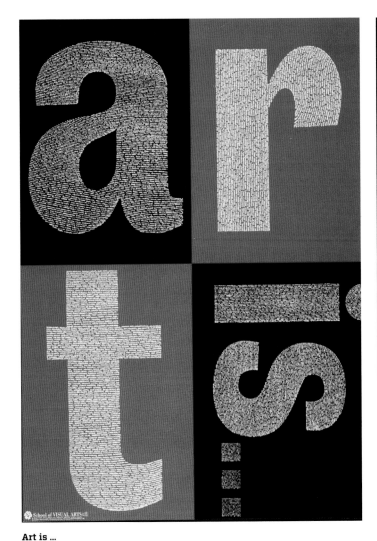

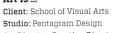

Art is …

Client: School of Visual Arts
Studio: Pentagram Design
Art Director, Creative Director, Designer: Paula Scher

The entertainment value of these posters for the School of Visual Arts are the collections of names scratched into the words *Art is…* Each is a famous or nearly famous artist—hence comprising what art is.

Fucking A

Client: The Public Theater
Studio: Pentagram Design
Art Director, Creative Director: Paula Scher
Designers: Paula Scher, Sean Carmody

"Fucking A" is Suzan-Lori Park's contemporary reshaping of *The Scarlet Letter*—now the A stands for abortion, rather than adultery.

Jazz in Willisau
Client: Jazz in Willisau
Designer: Niklaus Troxler

These posters by Niklaus Troxler have one thing in common: they are decidedly illegible at close range. They are abstract and expressionistic. And that visual strategy fits perfectly with the purpose of celebrating jazz.

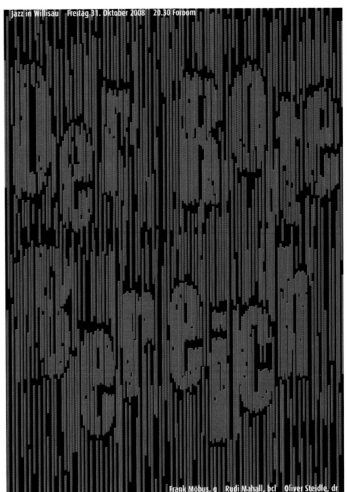

Tear Me Up

Client: *Creative Review*
Studio: Pentagram Design
Designer: Angus Hyland

This subscription campaign for *Creative Review*, the magazine covering creative communication, better be creative or the subscribers will disappear. Angus Hyland's bold headline inviting the reader to engage—and the payoff after engagement—is a demonstratively successful way of getting and holding interest.

Sommernachtstraum

Client: Od-Theater
Studio: Claudiabasel
Designers: Jiri Oplatek, Simon Stotz

Games are great entertainment, and this poster for the Od-Theater is a game to pick out the characters through the forest of type and pattern.

A Midsummer Night's Dream
Client: Shenkar College
Designer: Tamar Arieli

The work includes three posters. Tamar
Arieli used a scanner, leaves, and flowers
to illustrate a discussion between two
feminine characters from the play
A Midsummer Night's Dream.

Royal Shakespeare Company Stamps

Client: Royal Postal Service
Studio: johnson banks
Art Director, Designer: Michael Johnson

The johnson banks studio designed two new sets of stamps for the Royal Shakespeare Company, which were released to celebrate the theater company's fiftieth anniversary. The brief was to make them quite two distinctly different styles. The first set was collaborated with Marion Deuchars, illustrating key parts of the plays around dramatic photos from famous productions. They are almost like mini posters using words and images to reflect the plays. It's very unusual to have such a typographic set of stamps. The second is a mini "stage set," built with illustrator Rebecca Sutherland, which was shot with John Ross. This shows all the stages around Stratford, interspersed with characters and props from the plays.

LACK Magazine

Client: *LACK* Magazine
Studio: kissmiklos
Art Director, Designer: Miklós Kiss
Cover Photographer: Orsolya Hajas

LACK magazine is a Hungarian fashion magazine. Miklós Kiss designed a logo-type, which is classic like *VOGUE* but fresh and playful. Kiss says he "wanted to design a new progressive cover concept." He believed that most of the fashion magazines are boring: "There's always a photo and a name on it, and I wanted a more progressive and lively solution." He observed many times how the women hold the magazines in their hands and how often they get in inconvenient situations because they can't hold the magazines in a more comfortable way. He noticed that moving people potentially represent the best commercial. This was prompted by the idea of the cover as a handbag.

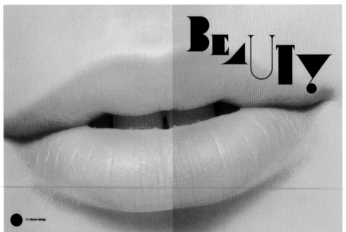

Extra!
**Shepherds rush to Bethlehem. Hear the news.
The Christmas Oratory at Nidaros Cathedral.**

Extra!
**Jesus found in manger. Hear the news.
The Christmas Oratory at Nidaros Cathedral.**

Extra!
**Herod scared. Plans mission. Hear the news.
The Christmas Oratory at Nidaros Cathedral.**

Christmas Oratorio
Client: Nidaros domkor/Trondheim Symphony Orchestra
Studio: HK Reklamebyrå
Designer: Stian Ward Bugten
Art Director: Stian Ward Bugten
Copywriter: Morten Rolseth
Account Executive: Frode Midjo
Project Manager: Mari Fosbæk Eriksen

What better way to recruit new audiences and
inspire established ones by importing the well-
known story of the Christmas Oratorio into a
newslike, eye-catching storytelling device.

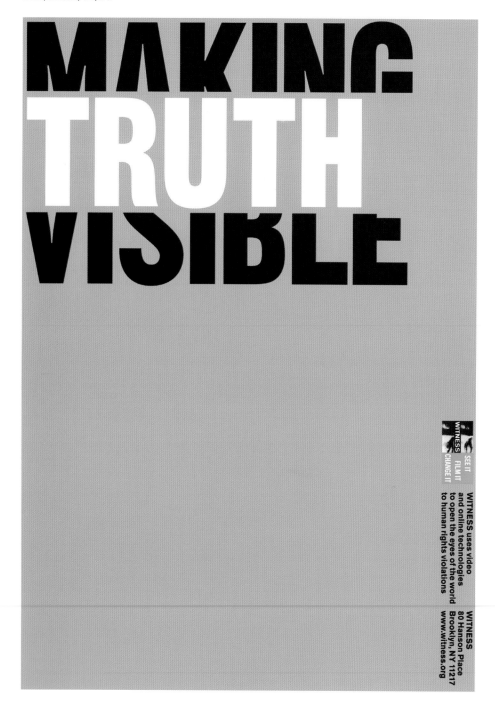

Street Shoes

Client: Street Shoes
Studio: Pentagram Design
Designers: Colin Forbes, Dan Friedman

The name *Street* had already been decided for a New York shoe store when Pentagram was commissioned to design a logotype. The identification of the shop is the graphic idiom of a traffic sign and was applied to shopping bags and stationery.

Making Truth Visible

Client: WITNESS
Studio: Pentagram Design
Designer: Harry Pearce

WITNESS is an international nonprofit organization that uses video to open the eyes of the world to human rights violations. Seeing the word *truth* emerge from the curtain of "making visible" powerfully suggests the idea of a witness.

Frida and Diego.
A Creative Love.

AGI project 2008 /
Leonardo Sonnoli

Frida and Diego. A Creative Love.
Client: AGI
Designer: Leonardo Sonnoli

Combining monumental type and miniscule
image grabs attention by virtue of the
unconventional scale.

Mom, I crashed your car…Life looks more beautiful when you are relaxed.
Client: New Look Spa
Studio: Fields—Brasília, Brazil
Art Director: Lucas Zaiden
Copywriter: Paulo Lima
Photographers, Illustrators, Typographers: Anderson Lisboa, Herbert Carlos

This campaign was created to promote a relaxation session at New Look Spa, located in Brasília. With the insight that people can deal better with bad situations when they are relaxed, the studio created sentences that usually freak people out, and framed them with soothing design typography.

Part Time Lover
Studio: André Beato
Art Director, Designer: André Beato

There is a lot to love in this typography. It looks like dark clouds, which implies the part-time nature of love. It is also black like a Cadillac, which suggests opulence.

Souvent tres Rythmées
Client: Steve Tomasula
Studio: Danny Warner Design
Art Director, Designer: Danny Warner

For a book spread, this is a visual interpretation of the meaning of the phrase, where visual fragmentation and rhythm are amplified through the letterform construction and expansion.

16 and Pregnant

Client: MTV Networks
Designer, Typographer: Stephen Byram
Art Director: Lance Rusoff

Simplicity is its own reward. In certain cases, like this logo, it can also have an entertainment component. Does the 6 look pregnant, or what?

MTV News

Client: MTV Networks
Designer, Typographer: Stephen Byram
Art Director: Lance Rusoff

The challenge here is to determine why these shapes are used for MTV News. They suggest people and talking, but in such an abstract way as to force a long ponder.

Cake

Client: Sony Music
Art Director, Designer, Illustrator, Typographer: Stephen Byram

Stephen Byram's comic character composed of type and image—both childlike and professional, original, and pastiche—provides enough humor to keep the viewer smiling.

fiction
film
conver-
music
sation
art

aprilmay98 $4.50

Speak, Issue 5 (Cover)
Client: *Speak*
Studio: Martin Venezky's Appetite Engineers
Designer: Martin Venezky
Art Director, Creative Director: Dan Rolleri (publisher and editor)
Photographer, Illustrator, Typographer: Darin Pappas
Type Designer: Henrik Kubel

artfictionmusic
fashionfilmconversation

spring97 $4.50

Speak, Issue 9 (cover)
Client: *Speak*
Studio: Martin Venezky's Appetite Engineers
Designer: Martin Venezky
Art Director, Creative Director: Dan Rolleri (publisher and editor)
Photographer, Illustrator, Typographer: Darin Pappas
Type Designer: Henrik Kubel

Magazine covers are meant to be entertaining. Martin Venezky's covers, from the cut logo to the images, are rooted in a surreal comedy, designed to pique attention and entertain.

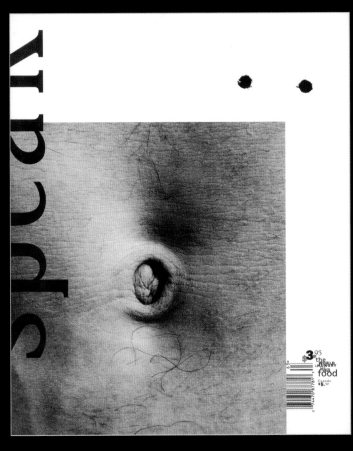

***Speak*, Issue 8 (cover)**
Client: *Speak*
Studio: Martin Venezky's Appetite Engineers
Designer: Martin Venezky
Art Director, Creative Director: Dan Rolleri (publisher and editor)
Photographer, Illustrator, Typographer: Darin Pappas
Type Designer: Henrik Kubel

***Speak*, Issue 3 (Cover)**
Client: *Speak*
Studio: Martin Venezky's Appetite Engineers
Designer: Martin Venezky
Art Director, Creative Director: Dan Rolleri (publisher and editor)
Photographer, Illustrator, Typographer: Darin Pappas
Type Designer: Henrik Kubel

Blackpool Pleasure Beach
Client: Blackpool Pleasure Beach
Studio: johnson banks
Designers: Michael Johnson, Kath Tudball,
Julia Woollams
Art Director, Creative Director: Michael Johnson

This identity scheme for a famous roller-
coaster park in North West England takes
the kinetic aspects of a theme park and
interprets them with type. The noises,
screams, ooohs, and aaahs that surround
a visitor are made integral to the park's
identity through their own unique triple-
width typeface and specially designed
typographic one-offs.

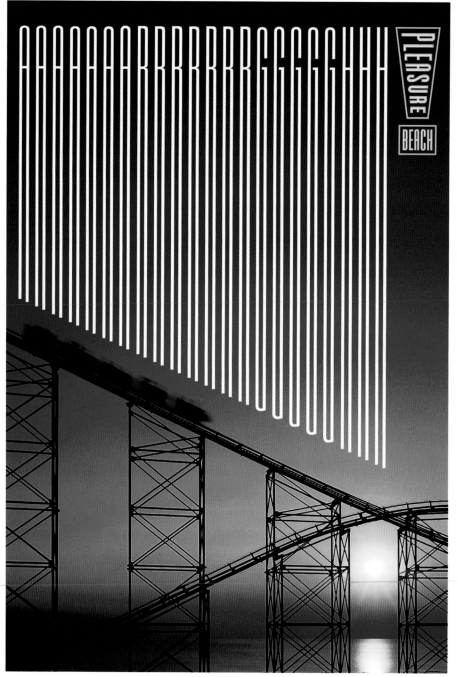

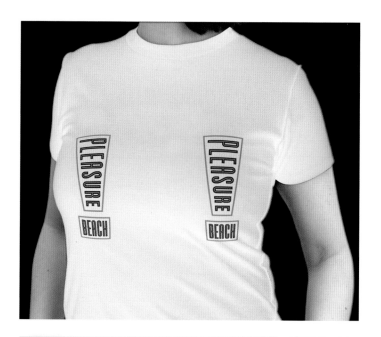

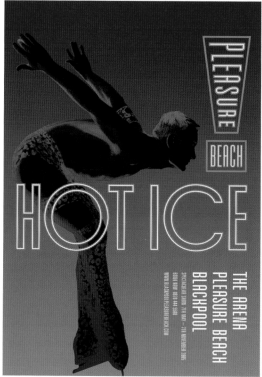

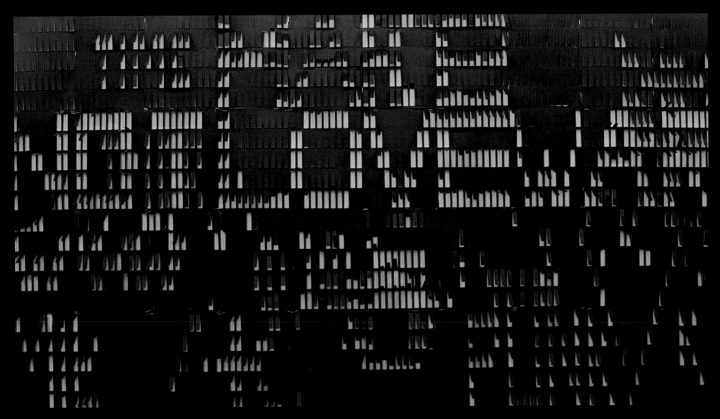

Tab Installation
Client: Graduate School Candidacy Research
Art Director, Designer: Cassie Hester

A tab instructs people to fold or tear. A wall of laser-cut tabs begs to be manipulated. "I installed this piece on the third floor of Pollack on March 8, around 5 p.m. I did not prefold/pretear any of the tabs, nor did I leave any instructions with the piece," says Cassie Hester. "I thought the initial start of the tab manipulation would be a slow one. I thought many would walk by it and possibly be intrigued, but ultimately feel uncomfortable/confused about the expectations until some brave soul took the plunge and folded and/or tore to begin the process. However, I arrived at Pollack at 9 a.m. the following day and students were already folding away."

Dig Deep
Client: Graduate School Candidacy Research
Art Director, Designer: Cassie Hester

Sign sequins are nailed 1 inch (2.5 cm) apart on a grid. Each sequin has a short straw spacer behind it that prevents it from resting directly against the board. The typographic message is created with reflected pink light. It is soon to be installed on the exterior of the Pollack Building at Virginia Commonwealth University in Richmond.

6

PHILOSOPHIZE

titilate

emōtē

EXPRESS

A manifesto should be a declaration of war against complacency. At the very least it should trigger thinking.

Spill your guts for all to see. That's expression! In recent years designers have promoted a trend of imposing personal expression on others through design manifestos. Not just post-it postcard-size statements about the wonders of existence, but posters, billboards, and monumental typographic installations with words of wisdom and observation—some critical others farcical, some hopeful others cynical. This may have started when in the 1980s Barbara Kruger and Jenny Holzer introduced type and image into their gallery and street art as means of conveying heady messages. Words were their ammunition. Sometimes they were aimed with pinpoint intelligence at social ills, other times they randomly sprayed the battlefield with personal expressions.

Design manifestos are produced at all conceptual levels and in all physical sizes, from simplicity to complexity. Designers who have made it their mission to save the world,

and even those who have less ambitious goals, routinely engage the environment in typographic installations that express their principles or state of mind. Often they are enigmas designed to make the passersby think about what it means to them. "You're Not My Type" (page 163) written large on an empty park gate, appears to be a message about human relations—or is it more enigmatically abstract? Is it about types of people or typographies? The interpretation is in the mind of the viewer.

A manifesto is a double-edged sword. It can articulate goals and desires in an honest and inspiring way. It can also be perceived as so much babble—pretentious at best—and best ignored. A true manifesto is an expression of personal truth and will make those who do not agree wince. And that's the point. A manifesto should be a declaration of war against complacency. At the very least it should trigger thinking.

Some of these typographic expressions are little more than fortune cookie exhortations. "Everyone Must Take Time to Sit and Watch the Leaves Turn" (page 166) has a greeting card cadence—and looks that way too. "Everything's Gonna Be Alright" (page 195) dug into the soil of a field and photographed from above, has the cookie sentiment but a more raw appearance. Conversely, "Hurry Up" (page 173), composed of huge bones hanging in a gallery space, or "Fail Harder" (page 181), painted on a large canvas in white on gray, have a more world-weary tone.

Universal expressions often begin as personal ones. Stefan Sagmeister's "Confidence Produces Fine Results" (page 176), a typographic installation made of green and yellow bananas that turn brown as they ripen, obliterating the message, offers a low-impact, decidedly self-interpretive message with resonance for many who receive it.

This manner of personal expression has also been co-opted by advertisers to sell a product. The billboard for Levi's (page 180), composed of three rows each with nine moving gears, with fragments of letterforms, which when lined up says "We Are All Workers," is a clever way of presenting a mystery and providing a "reveal," in the form of an empirical statement. *We Are All Workers* seems to imply that we are all in this (whatever *this* is) together and Levi's is the glue.

In terms of beauty, many of the expressions in this section are rendered with pristine elegance. "Conscience" (page 178) is written with dew drops on a leaf, "People" is formed by costumed Korean dancers holding semicircular fans, and "Good" and "Great" (page 179) are formed by red and yellow apples held up high by a procession of attractive girls dressed in white lace tops and golden skirts. Yet the most striking for its aesthetic richness and cultural significance is "Depends on Each Person" (page 178) designed as a wedding day henna tattoo on the hand of a young woman.

Expression in this typographic format will rarely be too lengthy. Too many words spoil the rhythm (and it is pedantic, too). The most effective are epigrams that read quickly yet linger in the consciousness. "You Don't Matter" (page 183), a sequence of expressive letterforms, is among the most haunting. But "Grow" (page 194), written in script made from moss, eloquently says it all.

Wild at Heart

Studio: Anna Garforth
Art Director, Designer, Photographer, Illustrator,
Typographer: Anna Garforth

"I woke up one day," says Garforth, "went for a run in the forest and then made this piece."

Explorers/Art Housed in Area Development

Client: Treaty of Utrecht
Studio: Autobahn
Designer: Autobahn
Photographer: Marieke Wijntjes

Tapewriter
Studio: Autobahn
Designer: Autobahn

Nature is such a resilient thing and, for designers, an opportunity to use new materials. This message is more impactful thanks to the unique approach to typography—and no pesky grass stains either.

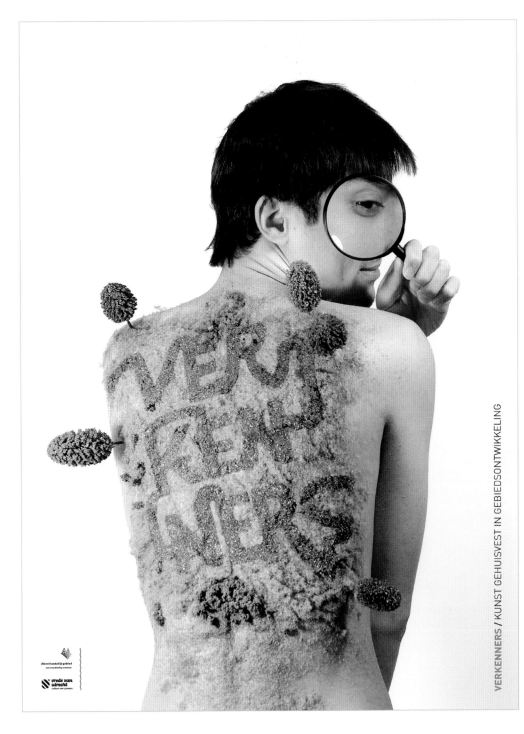

Explorers/Art Housed in Area Development
Client: Treaty of Utrecht
Studio: Autobahn
Designer: Autobahn
Photographer: Marieke Wijntjes

Arts In Area Development is a collaboration between artists and area developers. Together they are looking for a way to provide a place for art in areas yet to be developed. Autobahn made a small but congenial publication containing the answers to these questions and a presentation of the realized projects. The image concept of this booklet is inspired by the series *Landscapes* by photographer Levi van Veluw. In consultation with van Veluw, Autobahn has adopted this visual language to create a typographical cover image.

VERKENNERS / KUNST GEHUISVEST IN GEBIEDSONTWIKKELING

Everyone Must Take Time to Sit and Watch the Leaves Turn
Art Director, Designer: Evelin Kasikov

Stitched lettering is based on a quote by Elizabeth Lawrence: "Everyone must take time to sit and watch the leaves turn." Pixelated type is converted to laborious hand-embroidery. The piece consists of 15,588 stitches (two colors, 7,794 stitches each). The meditative, repetitive process of creating this work emphasizes the slow passage of time.

Cock Rock
Studio: Quiltsrÿche
Designer: Boo Davis

This 62 x 74-inch (1.6 x 1.9 m) quilt is made up of 1,147 squares. This one-patch variation expresses the timeless sentiment "Rock out with your cock out" in patchwork block letters.

Beastie
Studio: Quiltsrÿche
Designer: Boo Davis

Beastie features "God bless the children of the beast" spelled out with patchwork squares in a variation of a traditional Housetop design.

Sentences Wall Stickers and Posters
Studio: Harmonie intérieure
Art Director, Designer:
Fabien Barral

The Harmonie intérieure workshop grew from the experiences of Fabien and Frdérique Barral decorating their own home. Passionate about typography, they create collections, not only to decorate and harmonize, but also to send a message about your home, your personal space.

Squarepusher
Client: Karlstorbahnhof Heidelberg
Studio: GGGrafik
Art Director, Designer: Götz Gramlich

Designer Götz Gramlich pushed some squares in this poster for Squarepusher.

Zwischen den Zeilen Lesen
Client: "Mut zur Wut" Exhibition
Studio: GGGrafik
Art Director, Designer: Götz Gramlich

Götz Gramlich says, "In today's world of media saturation, we have all become too eager or too lazy to do anything else but accept everything at face value. The art of reading between lines, of hollowing out political and populist tirades, and exposing the hollowness of our politicians has gone lost. Society is increasingly being spoon-fed hate rants and sound bites, which have all been decontextualized. It's no coincidence that so many of my posters deal with issues and call on us to take a closer look. I get infuriated by false oversimplifications, which is why this poster is such an epiphany. I used Germany's tabloid newspaper the *Bild* as a background, and by chance I used the cover that caused a huge political stir with German politician Thilo Sarrazin's comments about the dumbing down of Germany due to immigrants failing to integrate."

Exhibition Poster: Niklaus Troxler Student Class Show
Studio: Visiotypen
Designers: Philipp Hubert, Sebastian Fischer

The Earth Will Give Birth to Her Death
Client: Anti Design Festival London
Studio: Visiotypen
Designer: Sarah Krebietke
Art Directors, Creative Directors: Philipp Hubert, Sebastian Fischer

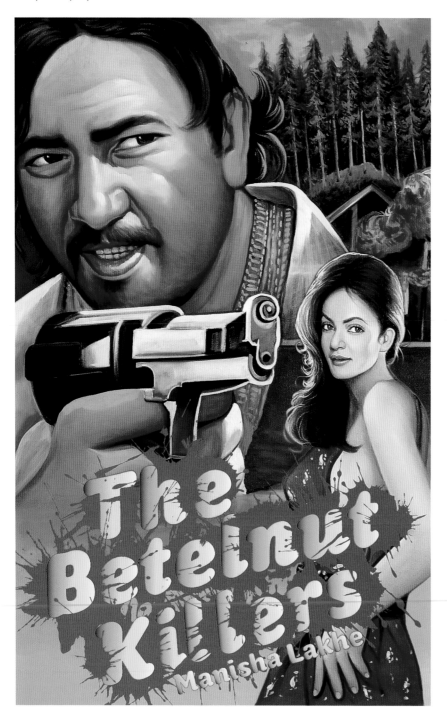

Communication
Studio: Ishan Khosla Design
Art Director, Designer: Ishan Khosla

Work in Progress for a Better Tomorrow
Studio: Ishan Khosla Design
Art Director, Designer: Ishan Khosla

The Betelnut Killers
Client: Random House
Studio: Ishan Khosla Design
Art Director, Designer: Ishan Khosla

The Betelnut Killers are notorious in India, the subject of a recent book and movie. This suggests the brutality of them and purposely triggers the viewer's fear factor.

Live/Love Postcards
Client: Chronicle Books
Studio: Studio AND
Art Director, Designer, Typographer: Jean-Benoit Levy
Publisher: Debra Lande

Through the use of the lenticular printing, two words interact, creating a visual wordplay. Each word is composed into colors that relate to its meaning and blend into each other as the words are changing. The visual effect of this image demonstrates the upcoming spirit of transforming surfaces.

**Nije da nije, ali nije ni da nije
(Definitely maybe)**
Client: Belgrade Summer Festival '08
Art Director; Designer: Jana Oršolić
Creative Director: Igor Oršolić
Produced by KIOSK contemporary art platform,
sponsored by ERSTE bank

A line from a poem by Srdjan Valajrevic.

**Moj život nije slican nicijem
(My life is unlike any other)**
Client: Belgrade Summer Festival '08
Art Director; Designer: Jana Oršolić
Creative Director: Igor Oršolić
Produced by KIOSK contemporary art platform,
sponsored by ERSTE bank

A line from a song by Goribor, a Serbian
blues-rock-thrash band, is translated
to English. The neon sign, a generally
engaging phenomenon mainly used for
commercial purposes, is transformed
here into an object of cultural content and
personal messaging.

Make Something
Client: Wieden+Kennedy
Agency: W+K 12.5
Design: W+K 12.3
Creative Director: Jelly Helm

What can be more engaging of the senses than the cacophony of letters and materials—dimensional, illuminated, and visceral—than this three-

Hurry Up/Slow Down
Client: Wieden+Kennedy
Agency: W+K 12
Design/Build: W+K 12.3
Creative Director: Jelly Helm

This installation of bones, suspended in the lobby of Wieden+Kennedy from clear monofilament, was completed in a single night. The night before the

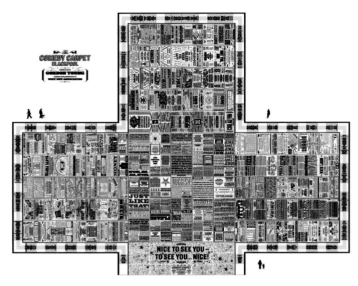

The Comedy Carpet, Blackpool, 2011
Client: Blackpool Council
Design: Gordon Young in collaboration with Why Not Associates

This "typographic artwork," commissioned and financed by The Blackpool Council and other development agencies, is a celebration of England's rich cultural heritage. It features monologues, gags, and catchphrases spoken by hundreds of British comedians. Lovingly transformed into a carpet of type, the expressions of comic spirits stretch over 1,720 square meters. Gordon Young and Andy Altman read countless writings by and about comedians for content and composed their statements in type that echoed classic English musical hall bills and posters. The letters, cut from granite, were created, incredibly, by a high-pressure water jet cutter. 180,000 individual red and black granite and blue cobalt concrete forms were ordered by hand. Each section of 2 x 4 meters, weighing four tons, was made from a mold. It took more than a year to source the materials. A dedicated factory was designated to manufacture the artwork. And a special concrete, which would "flow like cream into the counters of the letters," took months to develop. Along with the famous Blackpool Tower built in 1893 and influenced by the Eiffel Tower, The Comedy Carpert is literally the next great UK landmark.

Banana Wall
Client: Deitch Projects
Art Director: Stefan Sagmeister
Designers: Richard The, Joe Shouldice

At the opening of an exhibition at Deitch Projects in New York, the designers featured a wall of ten thousand bananas. Green bananas created a pattern against a background of yellow bananas spelling out the sentiment: self-confidence produces fine results. After a number of days the green bananas turned yellow and the type disappeared.

Standard Chartered Commercial
Client: Standard Chartered
Studio: Sagmeister Inc.
Agency: TBWA Asia Pacific, John Merrifield
Producers: Shareen Thumbo, Brian Francis
Art Director: Stefan Sagmeister
Designers: Joe Shouldice, Stephan Walter, Andrew Byrom
Production: Passion Pictures

This sixty-second commercial for the conservative (and socially conscious) bank Standard Chartered takes its typographic approach throughout Asia, Africa, and the Middle East.

We Are All Workers
Client: Len Peltier, Levi's
Studio: Sagmeister Inc.
Designer: Jessica Walsh
Production: Atomic Props

The Levi's billboard illustrates the notion of "We are all workers" by constantly breaking down and rebuilding the typography placed on actual turning cogwheels. New Yorkers loved the concept and many had themselves photographed in front of it.

Fail Harder
Client: Wieden+Kennedy
Agency: W+K 12
Design/build: W+K 12.3
Creative Director: Jelly Helm

This installation, made from over one hundred thousand clear
pushpins, was completed over a weekend as a surprise gift to
Wieden+Kennedy by students in the third year of its experimental
in-house school.

Lost Identity

Designers: Sebastian Cremers, Daniel Schludi

Based on a story by David Lynch that deals with the loss of identity, the designers created a three-dimensional typeface. Everybody who struggles through this "not knowing" can take those letter cubes and tell her or his own story.

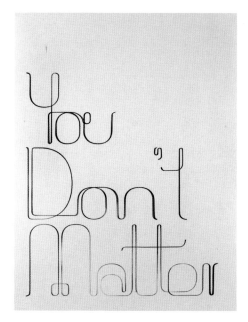

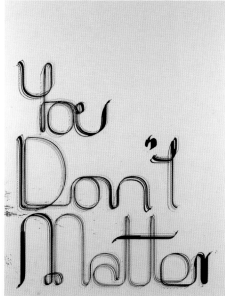

YDM02-YDM04
Studio: Blank
Designers: Martin Borst, Sebastian Cremers, Daniel Schludi

Martin Borst, Sebastian Cremers, and Daniel Schludi converted a plotting machine into an output device that can draw, scratch, or cut with almost any traditional drawing technique, in order to achieve aesthetics looking neither drawn by hand nor produced with only a computer. Most interesting and inspiring are all the little mistakes this machine makes, because of too much data, too much water, color, pressure, and so on. This expansion space describes the machine's actual identity. No image looks like the other.

Don't Shit On Me
Designer: Martin Borst

A poster, created with antipathy to pigeons.

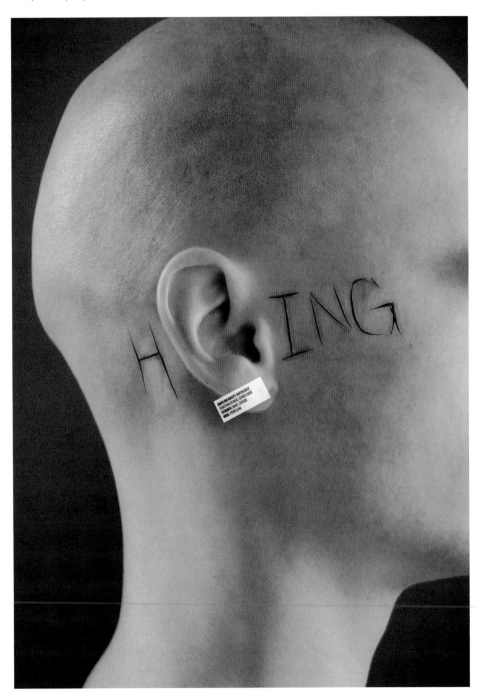

Hearing
Client: University of Media and Design Karlsruhe
Designers: Sebastian Cremers, Martin Borst
Photographer: Daniel Schludi
Model: Piero Glina

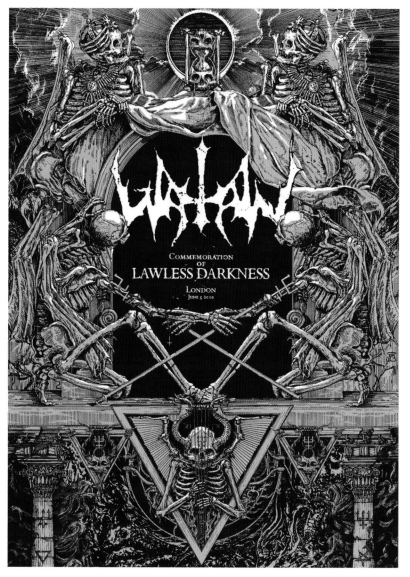

Commemoration of Lawless Darkness
Client: Watain
Studio: Metastazis
Art Director, Designer: Jean-Emmanuel "Valnoir" Simoulin
Additional Credit: Zbigniew M. Bielak

This poster was designed for the release party of Watain's *Lawless Darkness* album in London, June 5, 2010. The poster has been silkscreened with an ink made from human blood.

WAIT MORE.

STOP

FORGET HISTORY. IT'S NOT YOURS ANYMORE.

Wait More
Designer: Slavimir Stojanovic

Using international information graphics and symbols, the designer uses a verbal twist creating a visual pun.

Stop

History

STARS
MUD
GOLD

LIFE INSTRUC- TIONS ARE NOT AVAILABLE AT THE MOMENT.

EMPTY
FULL

Stars

Life Instructions

Empty

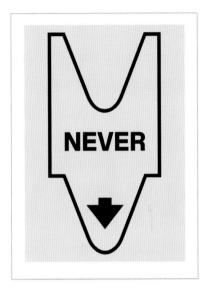

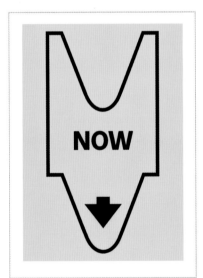

Never & Now
Designer: Leonardo Sonnoli with Irene Bacchi

In everyday life, the available time is always too long or too short. This poster toys with that notion.

Diritti Doveri (Rights and Obligations)
Designer: Leonardo Sonnoli

Poster for a conference on immigrant rights and obligations.

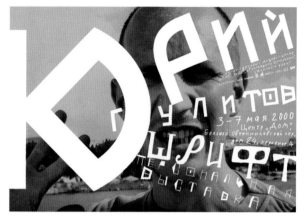

Yuri Gulitov—Typeface
Client: Solo Exhibition Poster
Art Director, Designer: Yuri Gulitov
Photographer: Ekaterina Gulitova

Poster for solo exhibition "Yuri Gulitov—Typeface."

They Are Just People, Only with Down Syndrome
Client: International Poster Campaign
Studio: Gulitovdesign
Designer: Yuri Gulitov

International poster campaign.

The Beach
Studio: Gulitovdesign
Designer: Yuri Gulitov

Poster for the "Painting Solo" exhibition.

In Other Words

Designers: Patrycja Zywert, Tobiasz Usewicz

This project is composed of a series of posters aiming to encourage people to use the actual language instead of text abbreviations, such as *LOL*, to make communication much richer and more human.

189

Daily Laundry by 3F Project
Art Directors, Designers: Ethan Park,
Changbae Seo
Coordinator: Yu Jin Lee

'Function Follows Form' is the main concept for the 3F Project. "The project tries to find new functions following the changing forms of ordinary subjects," say the designers.

Stylistic Gallery
Client: Stylistic Gallery
Art Director: Ethan Park
Photographer, Filmographer: Daniel Jon

Stylistic Gallery is a showcase for creative individuals and businesses to display and sell their work online.

SKY TV Rebranding Campaign
Client: Sky TV Italy
Agency: 1861 United
Art Director: Ethan Park
Art Coordinator: Dino Alladin
Photographer: Daniel Jon

The new campaign slogan "Free to" is accompanied by the key words *excited*, *exalted*, *choose*, and *flirt*, and is constructed entirely with objects.

Called Home
Art Director, Designer: Ethan Park
Photographer: Ethan Park

"When I was young, my mother used to say if I cried, my dad would have to go back to military service even though he had already been," says Ethan Park. So whenever Park cried thereafter he would call home to make sure that wasn't happening.

How I Can Touch Your Heart
Art Director, Designer: Ethan Park
Photographer: Ethan Park
Copywriter: Louise Shepherd

Ethan Park underscores his personal messages by making type and letters out of found objects. In this way he believes he can touch people's hearts.

Spoonful of Sugar

Studio: School of Visual Arts MFA Design
Art Director, Designer, Photographer: Leen Sadder

A hand-lettered umbrella is used in a campaign to cheer New Yorkers up on a rainy day through Mary Poppins.

Danny's Continental Cocktail Lounge

Client: Solo(s) Project House in Newark, New Jersey
Designer: Daniel Patrick Helmstetter
Photographers: Matt Kabel, Lynn Belles

Painted over the course of three long weeks in September of 2010, Danny's Continental Cocktail Lounge is a big bold ceiling-to-floor literary explosion—a poem that has painted its way off the page.

Grow
Studio: Anna Garforth
Art Director, Designer: Anna Garforth
Photographer, Illustrator, Typographer: Anna Garforth

Grow is one word in a sentence that will spell out, "Grow beyond what you know." The other words will be created in different hidden green spots around London. This message explores pushing the boundaries of what is expected.

Bite Off More Than You Can Chew
Studio: Anna Garforth
Art Director, Designer: Anna Garforth
Photographer, Illustrator, Typographer: Anna Garforth

A poster you can eat and reflect upon over a cup of tea, "Bite off more than you can chew" encourages the viewer to think outside of the box.

The Future
Client: Semi-Permanent
Studio: Mash
Designers: James Brown, Peta Kruger
Art Director: James Brown
Photographer: Dom Roberts
Illustrator, Typographer: Peta Kruger
Copywriter: David Kalucy
Model Talent: Leslie Lewis

Studio Mash was invited to create an image that depicted the concept of *future*. This piece was later published in *Semi-Permanent*, a book featuring design and illustration pieces from around the world. "At the time it was produced, everyone was talking about the environment and global warming (as we still are)," notes James Brown. "We wanted to convey some lighthearted humor, since most people have a gloomy/cynical outlook on the future."

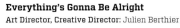

Everything's Gonna Be Alright
Art Director, Creative Director: Julien Berthier

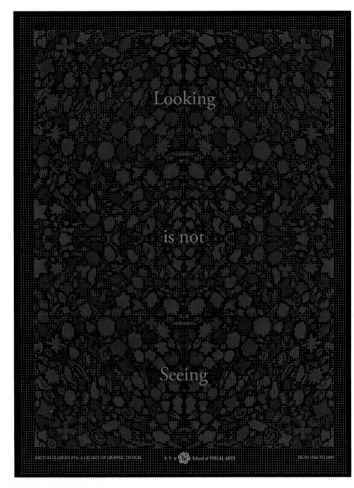

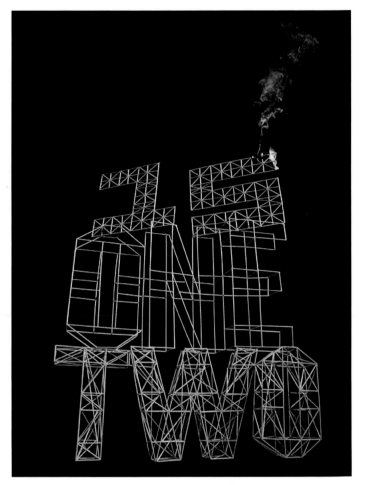

Looking Is Not Seeing
Client: School of Visual Arts
Designer: Milton Glaser

This poster celebrating Milton Glaser's show at the Visual Arts Gallery (September 2009) violates the fundamental rule of poster design. Above all, a poster must be visible. This poster deliberately challenges that assumption by being barely perceivable. "The message emerges only as a consequence of sustained observation," says Glaser. "After a few moments of staring at the poster, both the message and the color range become increasingly obvious. A miracle of perception? Perhaps."

WIRED
Client: *Wired* magazine
Designer: Stephen Doyle

Stephen Doyle uses three dimensions to ask a dimensional question. Whatever the answer, there is an inevitable doom in the offing as the wood framework of his words ignite in flame.

Pathos Floor Exibition

Art Director, Designer, Photographer: Nikola Puzigaca

"Pathos," reads the poster, "is one of the three modes of persuasion in rhetoric (along with ethos and logos). Pathos appeals to the audience's emotions." The wood cutout letters, leaning against the plaster wall, suggest the everyday nature of the word and the extraordinary responses people have through pathos.

7

LLUMINATE

EDIFY

IMP ART

EDUCATE

Graphic design arguably is itself a grand portal to the process of education.

Every day, every minute we are being educated. As long as information comes our way we are learning something. To *inform* implies to *educate*. Yet there is a fine line separating these two verbs. Not all information is truly educational; not all education relies entirely on information. While the goal may be the same (i.e., to encourage thinking and doing), the content and context of informing and educating is sometimes distinct.

Educational messages that provide information require an additional cognitive step. Translating the information imbedded in raw image and text into fuel that powers various behavioral and intellectual engines is the goal. How this is accomplished demands different steps depending on what is imparted.

What do we mean by, "Not all education relies on information"? Well, sometimes education can be triggered by designed signs and symbols, similar to those that tell us to *stop*, *go*, *do*. For example, the logo for we (page 200), which also cleverly transposes into me, is a mnemonic for an organization founded by U.S. vice president Al Gore to improve environmental education and ultimately action. While the mark is not loaded with data, it does symbolize a wealth of educational initiatives. So, in this sense the logo is a button that when literally and figuratively pressed opens a floodgate that helps educate people on important environmental issues.

Neither does the poster for 2011 Bridge (page 203), "Connect. Act. Transform," provide the data necessary to actually accomplish these stated behaviors. Rather, it is an announcement that hopefully will trigger the urge to learn more. In this way the goal of education is enabled.

Conversely, the McKinsey Conference booklet (page 202) is filled with loads of information, serving as a tutorial for where the global corporations in Switzerland can be found and what they do. For those who need to know more about Swiss finance and business, the mnemonic words used throughout this document are guides to the data.

"The Politics of Science" "Shame", and "Lies" (page 207) are metaphoric typographic illustrations that compress many visual ideas into the letters of the respective words. Given that one picture is worth a thousand words, these images may not provide facts and figures, but they enable the reader to immediately comprehend the essential theme of what is presented.

Given the same metaphoric principle, "It's Never Too Late To Get Where You're Going" (page 209) for the School of Visual Arts uses New York subway mosaics to signal that this is, in fact, a poster that appears in the New York subway stations. Another metaphoric approach, "The Person You Love is 72.8% Water" (page 204), a useful piece of information if there ever was one, is composed of lettering that literally illustrates the message.

Traditional type specimens are the epitome of educational messaging, for at once it must provide a literal showing and an aesthetic display of the typeface in question. The samples for Delvard Display (page 205) let the user know how to translate the information—type sizes and weights—into functional data.

Obviously, there are various ways to be educated through and by graphic design. Indeed graphic design arguably is itself a portal to education. Milton Glaser uses the phrase "to inform and delight" as a definition of what he does, and of design. Perhaps it is more accurate to say, "educate and delight," since that is the essence of this kind of creative activity.

We Logo
Client: Al Gore and the Alliance for Climate Protection
Agency: COLLINS: and The Martin Agency
Designers: John Moon, Mickey Pangilinan, Brian Collins, CCO
Art Director/Creative Directors: Ty Harper, Raymond McKinney, Sean Riley
Typographer: Chester Jenkins, Village

With time running out, Al Gore's Alliance for Climate Protection called on COLLINS: and The Martin Agency to "make solving the climate crisis everybody's business." Using the inspiration "We the People …" the team turns *me* into *we*, creating a transformational logo that calls the masses to action. Within months, hundreds of thousands call for a global treaty.

He/She Was Shot Dead Here
Designer: Mirna Hamady

These signs are at once deceiving and soothing. Aside from the image of a machine gun, the color suggests an entertainment zone rather than monuments to horror.

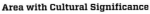

Area with Cultural Significance
Designer: Mirna Hamady

City War Museum
Designer: Mirna Hamady

Global Corporations in Switzerland

Client: McKinsey & Company
Studio: Mifflin-Schmid Design
Designer: Kaspar Schmid
Creative Director: Lize Mifflin
Illustrator: Mayo Bucher

Emphasizing words through demonstrative typography is one fast way to engage the reader and keep them wanting to read more copy, if only to learn the implication of the words.

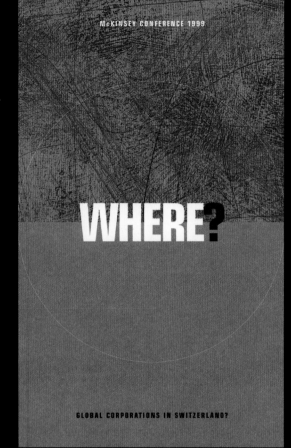

McKINSEY CONFERENCE 1999

WHERE?

GLOBAL CORPORATIONS IN SWITZERLAND?

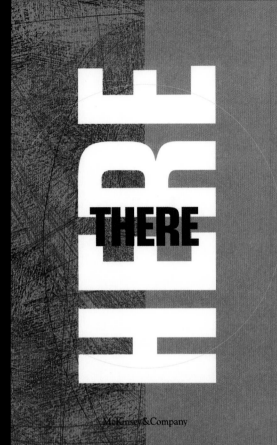

HERE THERE

McKinsey&Company

SPACE TIME

STOP GO!

SHAPE

2011 Bridge Conference

Client: School's Out Washington
Studio: Weather Control
Art Director, Designer: Josh Oakley

The Bridge From School to Afterschool and Back (or "Bridge Conference" for short) is an annual conference for afterschool and youth development professionals in the Pacific Northwest. With a background illustration displaying a cornucopia of Seattle icons and afterschool activities, the title of the 2011 conference—"Connect. Act. Transform."—needed to serve as a counterweight to the busyness of everything else.

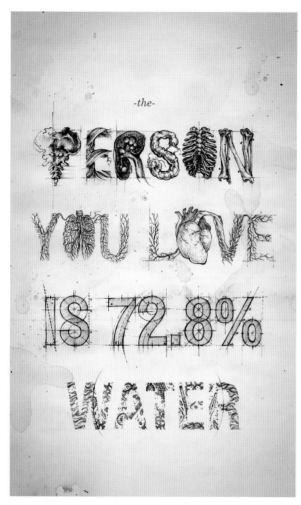

The Person You Love Is 72.8% Water
Designer: Teagan White

It is widely reported in school texts that the human body is largely composed of water. This poster is a twist on that statistic. The lettering ironically illustrates the ideas of body, love, formula, and liquid.

Less Is More
Studio: Bubadesign - Imagine unimaginable
Art Director, Designer: Todorović Ljubomir

This composition is asymmetrical and the letters are forming a kind of object or a shape. Todorović Ljubomir used wrinkled paper texture on letters, and black wood for the background. The logo of the project is *T* in a color drop and it represents the word *typography*. The slogan is, "Typography is beautiful if less is more."

Delvard Display Type Family
Client: Typonine
Studio: Typonine
Art Director, Designer: Nikola Djurek

Delvard Display is a series of six display
fonts: Display One through Five, and Fat,
for setting vivid, forceful, or saucy strings
of text. It offers a matching weight
system that allows same stems (weight)
throughout all styles and sizes.

Proportions
Proportions
Proportions
Proportions
Proportions

with matching weights system

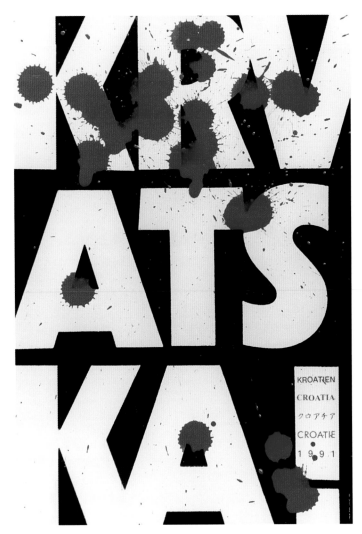

Čitajte između redova!" (Read beetwen the lines!)
Client: The City of Vukovar in exile
Studio: STUDIO INTERNATIONAL
Art Director, Designer: Boris Ljubičić

KRV-ATSKA!
Client: STUDIO INTERNATIONAL
Studio: STUDIO INTERNATIONAL
Art Director, Designer: Boris Ljubičić

The posters are meant to remind the viewer of aggression against Croatia. The title *KRV-ATSKA!* is derived from the Croatian word for *CROATIA: HRVATSKA*, the initial three letters forming another word, KRV (meaning "blood," in Croatian).

This poster beckons the viewer to come closer to learn the truth, explains Boris Ljubičić. The text between the lines was written by the people of Vukovar, "and my task was to communicate it to a wider public," he adds. "Modest, quiet, and with limited color, this work presents the truth without pathetic, patriotic, rhetorical, or political effects. I conceived, designed, and printed it on my own initiative since it was not in the spirit of official policy. Nevertheless, it was greatly appreciated by the people and was reprinted in several editions."

Shame

Client: *Village Voice*
Studio: Attic Child Press, Inc.
Designer: Minh Uong
Art Director, Creative Director: Ted Keller
Illustrator: Viktor Koen

Viktor Koen's choice of provocative imagery is composed in such a way as to make reading the word a terrifyingly cautionary experience.

Lies

Client: *Village Voice*
Studio: Attic Child Press, Inc.
Designer: Minh Uong
Art Director, Creative Director: Ted Keller
Illustrator: Viktor Koen

Viktor Koen is known for making surreal, indeed sci-fi collages out of disparate yet frightening materials. Lies, made from weaponry old and new, gives the word horrifying resonance.

The Politics of Science

Client: *New York Times Book Review*
Studio: AtticChild Press, Inc.
Designer, Illustrator: Viktor Koen
Art Director: Steven Heller

Viktor Koen's letters double as illustrations for the idea of science, adding a level of comprehension that is impossible to achieve with traditional type alone.

SVA Subway Poster
Designer, Illustrator: Mirko Ilić
Art Director: Michael Walsh
Creative Director: Anthony Rhodes

At first glance this poster with the title "To Help See Possibilities," promoting the School of Visual Arts, reads like any conventional typographic missive. Up close, however, the viewer learns it is made from toy soldiers, proving that seeing is really an intense act of consciousness.

SVA Subway Poster
Client: School of Visual Arts
Studio: Louise Fili Ltd
Designers: Louise Fili, John Passafiume, Dana Tanamachi
Art Director: Louise Fili
Creative Director: Anthony Rhodes

This poster is an homage to the urban mosaic artisans of the early twentieth century, created tile by tile, over weeks of painstaking Photoshop work. It serves as a wayfinding sign and a lesson in city iconography.

IT'S NEVER TOO LATE TO GET WHERE YOU'RE GOING

SCHOOL OF VISUAL ARTS

8

ALTƎR

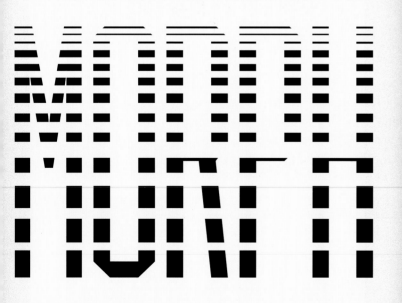

PROPOGATE PROPOGATE PROPOGATE PRO
POGATE PROPOGATE PROPOGATE PROPOG
GATE PROPOGATE PROPOGATE PROPOGATE
PROPOGATE PROPOGATE PROPOGATE PRO
PROPOGATE PROPOGATE PROPOGATE PRO
POGATE PROPOGATE PROPOGATE PROPOG
OGATE PROPOGATE PROPOGATE PROPOGA
PROPOGATE PROPOGATE PROPOGATE PRC
POGATE PROPOGATE PROPOGATE PROPOG
TE PROPOGATE   PROPOGATE P
GATE PROPOGATE PROPOGATE PROPOGAT
PROPOGATE PROPOGATE PROPOGATE PRO
POGATE PROPOGATE PROPOGATE PROPOG
GATE PROPOGATE PROPOGATE PROPOGAT
PROPOGATE PROPOGATE PROPOGATE PRO
OGATE PROPOGATE PROPOGATE PROPOGA
PROPOGATE PROPOGATE PROPOGATE PRO
POGATE PROPOGATE PROPOGATE PROPOG
GATE PROPOGATE PROPOGATE PROPOGAT
PROPOGATE PROPOGATE PROPOGATE PRO
E PROPOGATE PROPOGATE PROPOGATE P
OGATE PROPOGATE PROPOGATE PROPOGA

TRANSFORM

Transformation is not more than making the real abstract and vice versa. It is about taking something familiar and making it serendipitous.

Plus ça change. Changing personal attitudes and beliefs, working and living habits are transformative experiences. Occasionally, a particular work of art can become a trigger or serve as catalyst for transformation. Historically, this has occurred often through music, dance, writing, and painting. Perhaps less so with commercial art and design—but never say never. For different individuals, certain graphic designs or typographic treatments have transformed the ways design is perceived and practiced. Great influences derive from many, often surprising sources.

Graphic designers are used to being transformed and transforming as well. The field is constantly in flux. Moreover, design is to a large extent routinely manipulating form in order to break down the internal cognitive barriers that protect the brain from overloading on messages. It takes a keen design "thinker" to invent ways to bypass the internal filter and reach the mind with the message. Most everyday design fails to be so intrinsically able to transcend the barricades and, therefore, transform behavior.

Survival of the fittest is as true for graphic design as it is for animal species. If a message is not distinct and unique enough, it will never enter the consciousness. That's exactly where graphic design transformation is most useful as a communications tool. If the receiver perceives one thing but is "ambushed" by another, the chance of piquing attention—and emotion—is greater than a neutral presentation of the same message. While this may seem obvious, designers are not always aware of their potential power.

Intuitively tweaking design elements into stop and go signals is hardwired into anyone who claims the mantle of designer. Sometimes these are just matter of fact; others are deliberate detours around imposed rules and regulations.

This book is American- and Euro-centric, with the large number of typefaces and letterforms derived from the Latin alphabet. But a generous amount of Asian and Arabic designers are also included, many in this particular section, not because the language is incomprehensible but owing to the fact that more restrictions—not just political and social but cultural—hamper fluid design. Many of the designs in this section transform difficult calligraphic styles into designs that at once retain centuries-old traditions yet acknowledge their twentieth and twenty-first century origins.

The announcement for architecture professor Janusz Rębielak for CEAT in Iran (page 217) is a transformation of architectural schematic into a curiously abstract composition that suggests both Farsi lettering and architectural rendering. Combining the English and Farsi text serves as both information and texture for this stark black-and-white composition.

In a similar blending of two cultures, the black-and-white poster for the First Fadjr International Visual Arts Festival (page 219) is a transformation of what could have been an ordinary announcement into a dynamic, decorative alphabetic design.

Transformation is not more than making the real abstract and vice versa. It is about taking something familiar and making it serendipitous. Or even taking two things familiar and devising a third. The atypical typeface promotion (page 221) for Caslon Italic, Clarendon Bold, Helvetica Bold, and Carousel Medium uses familiar diacritical, punctuation, and numbers to transform a woman's face. The type forms become typographic clown masks that draw the eye to the face and faces.

Transformation is achieved in so many ways, but the most conventional graphic design method is The Decemberists (page 213) where the roots of a vine materialize as the title of the play. This approach is not merely common, it is enjoyable for the eye—a transformative game that requires little to decipher but packs a wallop when it is.

The Decemberists
with Justin Townes Earle

April 25, 2011
Calvin College
Grand Rapids, MI

Artwork by Sean Freeman

The Decemberists
Client: Stu Smith/Red Light Management
Art Director, Designer, Illustrator: Sean Freeman

The visual pun here is what makes this one of the most memorable logos or brands. Once deciphered, the vines of lettering wrap around cognition better than any unfettered font.

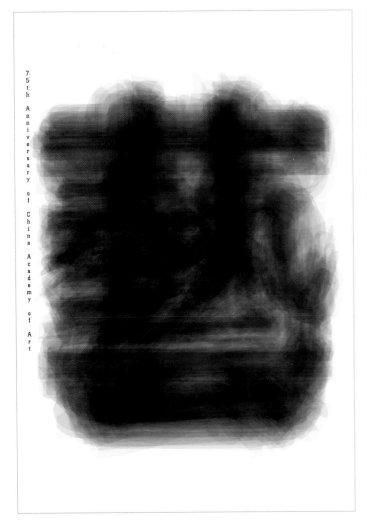

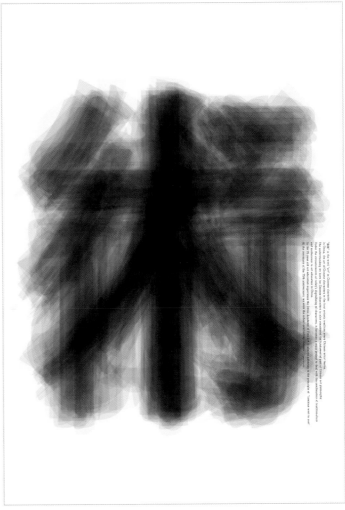

Seventy-Fifth Anniversary of China Academy of Art
Client: China Academy of Art, Hangzhou
Studio: Hesign
Art Director, Designer: Jianping He

This Chinese character means "art." China Academy of
Art celebrated its seventy-fifth anniversary in 2003.

New Graphic
Client: New Graphic Editorial, Nanjing China
Studio: Hesign
Art Director, Designer: Jianping He

Poster for the Chinese graphic magazine *New Graphic* in Nanjing, China.

China Image
Client: Taiwan Poster Design Association
Photo by Yin Jiang (Beijing) 2006

Poster for the Taiwan Poster Design Association.

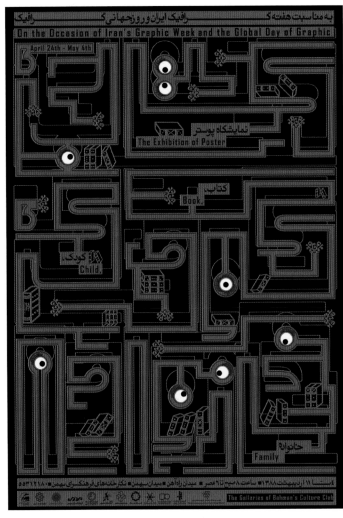

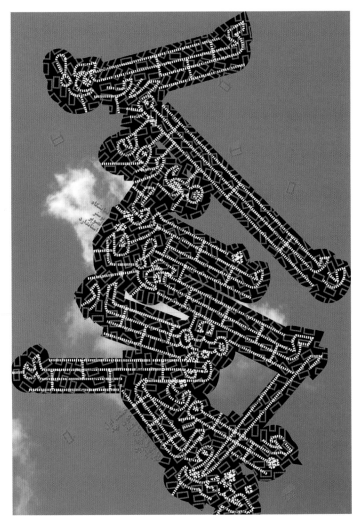

Book, Child, Family
Client: Iranian Graphic Designers Society (IGDS)
Studio: Amir Beik Studio
Art Director, Designer: Amir Hossein Ghoochibeik

Little is more successfully engaging than a graphic game—interactivity. This poster transforms the calligraphic forms into a labyrinth that pulls the viewer from here to there.

If you establish something wrong from the beginning it goes wrong up to the end.
Client: Rang Online Magazine
Studio: Amir Beik Studio
Art Director, Designer: Amir Hossein Ghoochibeik

On this poster, which was ordered by Standard institute in Iran for its festival, an old Iranian proverb inspired the designer.

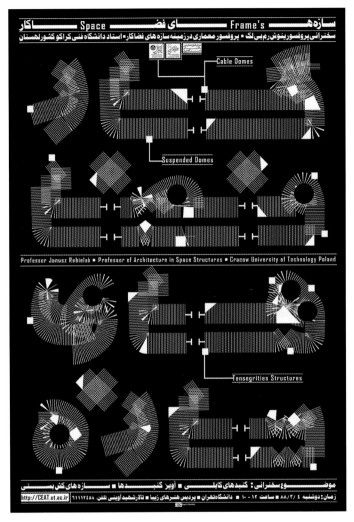

Ladies Only. No Men Are Allowed.
Client: Atashzad Art Gallery
Studio: Amir Beik Studio
Art Director, Designer: Amir Hossein Ghoochibeik

There is a distinct DIY punk quality to this pixelated exhibition poster that may not illustrate what's on exhibition, but demands the sense to go straight to the bull's-eye in the middle.

Space Frames
Client: Fine Arts Faculty of University of Tehran
Studio: Amir Beik Studio
Art Director, Designer: Amir Hossein Ghoochibeik

Is it architectural schematic or calligraphy? To the Western eye it is a uniquely and aesthetically pleasingly layering of elements, simply printed in black and white, that invites lengthy attention.

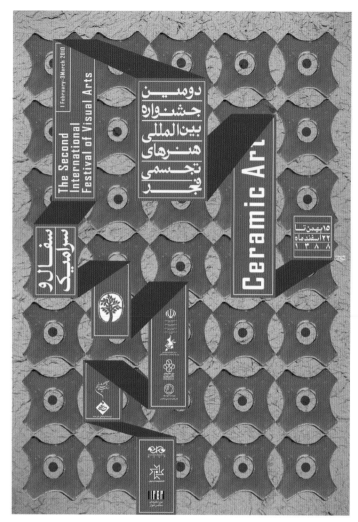

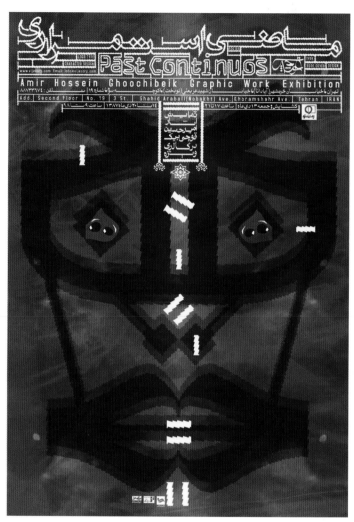

Vertical Letter
Studio: Amir Beik Studio
Art Director, Designer: Amir Hossein Ghoochibeik

From a Western perspective the calligraphic focal image is more than a literal message; it is an exquisite ornamental design that also is something of an anthropomorphic figure speaking the information.

Past Continuos
Studio: Amir Beik Studio
Art Director, Designer: Amir Hossein Ghoochibeik

The calligraphic mask at the center of this exhibition poster for Amir Hossein Ghoochibeik Graphic Work Exhibition (in Vejeh Galler) looks directly, albeit abstractly, into the eye of the viewer—demanding attention is paid.

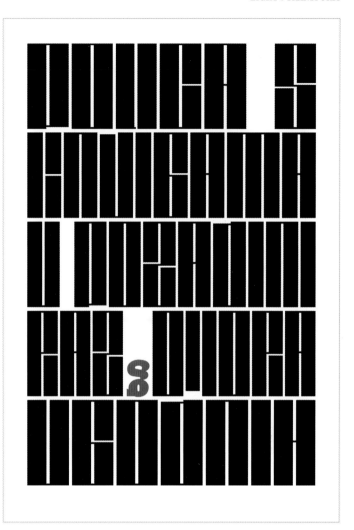

The First Fadjr International Visual Arts Festival
Client: Tehran Museum of Contemporary Art
Studio: Amir Beik Studio
Art Director, Designer: Amir Hossein Ghoochibeik

The hypnotic patterning of this Farsi calligraphy in its chaotic and unraveled state beckons the viewer to decipher and comprehend.

Polica sa knjigama/Bookshelf
Client: Nikola Djurek
Designer: Dejan Dragosavac Ruta

This poster uses Nikola's Meandar typeface to suggest the image of bookshelves. The text reads, "Polica s knjigama u pozadini razgovra ugodnih," which means, "Bookshelves in the background of pleasant conversations."

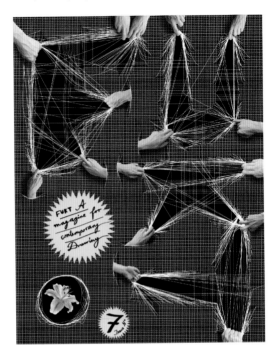

**FUKT Magazine
for Contemporary
Drawing #7**
Client: Björn Hegardt
(Editor, *FUKT Magazine*)
Studio: Ariane Spanier
Graphic Design
Designer: Ariane Spanier

Transforming a torn and
curled paper into the
letters of the magazine
logo

**FUKT Magazine
for Contemporary
Drawing #71/2**
Client: Björn Hegardt
(Editor, *FUKT Magazine*)
Studio: Ariane Spanier
Graphic Design
Designer: Ariane Spanier

Transforming hair into
the letters of the magazine
logo

FUKT Magazine for Contemporary Drawing #8/9
Client: Björn Hegardt (Editor, *FUKT Magazine*)
Studio: Ariane Spanier Graphic Design
Designer: Ariane Spanier

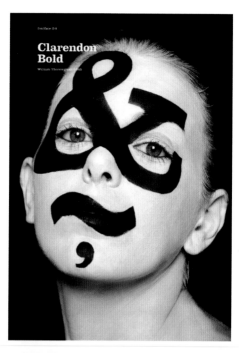

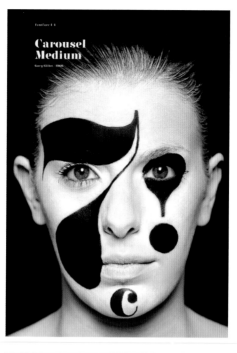

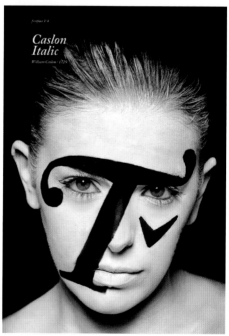

Fontface
Client: atipo
Studio: atipo
Art Director, Designer: atipo

Members of the atipo selected four typefaces from four outstanding type designers and combined the expression of gesture and text, while taking a brief journey through the type history. "Coming from an old style Roman, like Caslon, going through a slab serif, like Clarendon, a grotesque, like Helvetica, to Didone, like Carousel. We chose the characters that summarize the main features of each typeface, and most importantly, they operated as a mask on the model's face," the designer explains.

Job, Rave, Work
Designer: Alexander Shields
Art Director, Creative Director, Typographer: Alexander Shields
Photographers: Alexander Shields, William Eckersley
Additional Credit: Jimmy Turrell

God

Art Director, Designer, Typographer:
Alexander Shields
Photographers: Alexander Shields,
William Eckersley

These type sculptures were created
in various abandoned spaces across
London. The large type was constructed
using materials found in situ and the
chosen words reflect some aspect of the
abandoned space. After construction,
each piece was photographed using a
large-format, 5 x 4 camera. Words as
environmental fixtures (or monuments)
are among the best tools for impressing a
message, thought, or dictum on the mass
consciousness. These environmental
installations use the environment and
monumentalism to accomplish the deed.

ACKNOWLEDGMENTS

We are grateful to Emily Potts, our editor, for her continued support and encouragement. Thanks also to Winnie Prentiss, publisher, and Regina Grenier, art director at Rockport Publishers. Much appreciation to Rick Landers for the design of the book. Very special thanks to our research associates at Mirko Ilić Corp: Agnieszka Mielczarek-Orzylowski and Jee-eun Lee. And tips of the hat to Farhan Ajram, Jean Shim, Ahmed Elmadah, Itohan Edoloyi, Nikola Djurek, Dejan Krsic, Borut Vild, Krzysztof Dydo. And thanks to Alissa Cyphers, our copyeditor.

Thanks also to the international array of designers, illustrators, photographers, typographers, and art directors who have allowed us to use their work in this book as examples of what makes us Stop, Think, Go, and Do!

—Steven Heller & Mirko Ilić

ABOUT THE AUTHORS

Steven Heller is the cochair of MFA Design (Designer as Author + Entrepreneur) at the School of Visual Arts in New York and the cofounder of MFA Design Criticism, MFA Interaction Design, MPS Branding, and MFA Products of Design. He is the "Visuals" columnist of the *New York Times Book Review*, the "Graphic Content" columnist for *New York Times T-Style*, and he writes a column for the *Atlantic Magazine's* "Life" section. He is the author or editor of more than 135 books, contributor to *Eye*, *Print*, and *Baseline*, and writes The Daily Heller blog. He is the recipient of the 1999 AIGA Medal for Lifetime Achievement and the 2011 National Design Award "Design Mind."

Mirko Ilić is founder of Mirko Ilić Corp. in New York City. He has received medals from Society of Illustrators, Society of Publication Designers, Art Directors Club, *I.D.* magazine, and Society of Newspaper Design. Ilić is coauthor of *The Anatomy of Design* with Steven Heller and coauthor of *The Design of Dissent* with Milton Glaser.